## ALEXI KAYE CAMPBELL

Alexi Kaye Campbell's other plays include *The Pride* (Royal Court, London, 2008; Lucille Lortel Theatre, New York, 2010; Crucible Theatre, Sheffield, 2011; Trafalgar Studios, 2013); *Apologia* (Bush Theatre, London, 2009); *The Faith Machine* (Royal Court, London, 2011) and *Bracken Moor* (Shared Experience at the Tricycle Theatre, London, 2013).

*The Pride* received the Critics' Circle Award for Most Promising Playwright and the John Whiting Award for Best New Play. The production was also awarded the Laurence Olivier Award for Outstanding Achievement in an Affiliate Theatre.

His work for film includes *Woman in Gold* (BBC Films and Origin Pictures, 2015).

**Other Titles in this Series**

Annie Baker
THE FLICK

Mike Bartlett
BULL
GAME
AN INTERVENTION
KING CHARLES III
WILD

Stephen Beresford
THE LAST OF THE HAUSSMANS

Jez Butterworth
JERUSALEM
JEZ BUTTERWORTH PLAYS: ONE
MOJO
THE NIGHT HERON
PARLOUR SONG
THE RIVER
THE WINTERLING

Alexi Kaye Campbell
APOLOGIA
BRACKEN MOOR
THE FAITH MACHINE
THE PRIDE

Caryl Churchill
BLUE HEART
CHURCHILL PLAYS: THREE
CHURCHILL PLAYS: FOUR
CHURCHILL: SHORTS
CLOUD NINE
DING DONG THE WICKED
A DREAM PLAY *after* Strindberg
DRUNK ENOUGH TO SAY
    I LOVE YOU?
ESCAPED ALONE
FAR AWAY
HERE WE GO
HOTEL
ICECREAM
LIGHT SHINING IN
    BUCKINGHAMSHIRE
LOVE AND INFORMATION
MAD FOREST
A NUMBER
SEVEN JEWISH CHILDREN
THE SKRIKER
THIS IS A CHAIR
THYESTES *after* Seneca
TRAPS

debbie tucker green
BORN BAD
DIRTY BUTTERFLY
HANG
NUT
RANDOM
STONING MARY
TRADE & GENERATIONS
TRUTH AND RECONCILIATION

Anna Jordan
CHICKEN SHOP
FREAK
YEN

Lucy Kirkwood
BEAUTY AND THE BEAST
    *with* Katie Mitchell
BLOODY WIMMIN
CHIMERICA
HEDDA *after* Ibsen
IT FELT EMPTY WHEN THE
    HEART WENT AT FIRST BUT
    IT IS ALRIGHT NOW
NSFW
TINDERBOX

David Lindsay-Abaire
GOOD PEOPLE
RABBIT HOLE

Cordelia Lynn
LELA & CO.

Conor McPherson
DUBLIN CAROL
McPHERSON PLAYS: ONE
McPHERSON PLAYS: TWO
McPHERSON PLAYS: THREE
THE NIGHT ALIVE
PORT AUTHORITY
THE SEAFARER
SHINING CITY
THE VEIL
THE WEIR

Jack Thorne
2ND MAY 1997
BUNNY
BURYING YOUR BROTHER IN THE
PAVEMENT
HOPE
JACK THORNE PLAYS: ONE
LET THE RIGHT ONE IN
    *after* John Ajvide Lindqvist
MYDIDAE
STACY & FANNY AND FAGGOT
WHEN YOU CURE ME

Enda Walsh
BALLYTURK
BEDBOUND & MISTERMAN
DELIRIUM
DISCO PIGS & SUCKING DUBLIN
ENDA WALSH PLAYS: ONE
ENDA WALSH PLAYS: TWO
MISTERMAN
THE NEW ELECTRIC BALLROOM
ONCE
PENELOPE
THE SMALL THINGS
ROALD DAHL'S THE TWITS
THE WALWORTH FARCE

Alexi Kaye Campbell

# SUNSET AT THE VILLA THALIA

## NICK HERN BOOKS

London

www.nickhernbooks.co.uk

**A Nick Hern Book**

*Sunset at the Villa Thalia* first published in Great Britain as a paperback original in 2016 by Nick Hern Books Limited, The Glasshouse, 49a Goldhawk Road, London W12 8QP

*Sunset at the Villa Thalia* copyright © 2016 Alexi Kaye Campbell

Alexi Kaye Campbell has asserted his right to be identified as the author of this work

Cover image: original photography by Hayden Williams

Designed and typeset by Nick Hern Books, London
Printed in Great Britain by CPI Group (UK) Ltd

A CIP catalogue record for this book is available from the British Library

ISBN   978 1 84842 496 8

*Sunset at the Villa Thalia* was first performed in the Dorfman auditorium of the National Theatre, London, on 1 June 2016 (previews from 25 May). The cast was as follows:

| | |
|---|---|
| THEO | Sam Crane |
| CHARLOTTE | Pippa Nixon |
| HARVEY | Ben Miles |
| JUNE | Elizabeth McGovern |
| MARIA | Glykeria Dimou |
| STAMATIS | Christos Callow |
| ADRIAN | Thomas Berry/Billy Marlow/ Ethan Rouse |
| ROSALIND | Sophia Ally/Dixie Egerickx/ Scarlett Nunes |
| AGAPE | Eve Polycarpou |
| *Director* | Simon Godwin |
| *Designer* | Hildegard Bechtler |
| *Lighting Designer* | Natasha Chivers |
| *Music* | Michael Bruce |
| *Movement Director* | Jonathan Goddard |
| *Sound Designer* | Tom Gibbons |
| *Company Voice Work* | Jeannette Nelson |
| *Dialect Coach* | Charmian Hoare |
| *Staff Director* | Caroline Williams |

**Acknowledgements**

With thanks to Maria Stathakopoulou, Susan Powell, Marianna Fanshawe, Sandra Robinson, Vasilis Karathanos, Stathis Garifallos, Anastasia Ravi, Sebastian Born, Ben Power, and everyone at the National Theatre Studio.

*A. K.C.*

*To*
*Laurie*
*Stelios*
*Markos*
*με αγαπη*

**Characters**

THEO, *English, in his thirties, then forties*
CHARLOTTE, *English, in her thirties, then forties*
HARVEY, *American, in his forties, then fifties*
JUNE, *American, in her forties, then fifties*
MARIA, *Greek, seventeen*
STAMATIS, *Greek, in his fifties*
ADRIAN, *English, eight years old*
ROSALIND, *English, seven years old*
AGAPE, *Greek, in her sixties or seventies*

**Note on Play**

The play takes place in two different time periods:

April, 1967
August, 1976

The play takes place entirely on the terrace of a small house on the island of Skiathos, Greece.

*This text went to press before the end of rehearsals and so may differ slightly from the play as performed.*

**ACT ONE**

*The terrace of a simple peasant cottage in Greece, on the island of Skiathos. The few pieces of furniture which are scattered around the space are genuinely rustic, the furniture that a local Greek family would have used.*

*Somewhere on stage there is a small table with a chair in front of it. On the table there is an old Corona typewriter and a typed manuscript by its side, with a large stone placed on it to prevent the loose pages from blowing away.*

*It is early evening in April, 1967.*

THEO *stands on the terrace, dressed casually in slacks and an open-neck shirt, sandals. He stares out at the sea, and the sunset.*

THEO *is a dreamer.*

CHARLOTTE (*offstage*). Theo!

> CHARLOTTE *emerges from the house. She is dressed in a simple but bohemian style of the period. She is carrying two small wooden chairs and seems slightly flustered.*

> There's only whisky and something Greek that smells lethal.

THEO. He seemed like the whisky type. And she'll drink lighter fluid. She got through that bottle of retsina on the port as if it were water.

CHARLOTTE. There's Greek folk music on the radio, it's quite pleasant in a plaintive sort of way. Why are you just standing there?

THEO. Oh, you know, trying to think where it should go next, that kind of thing.

CHARLOTTE. They can sit on these. I found them in the basement.

THEO *notices she's carrying the chairs and goes to her, takes them from her.*

THEO. I could have fetched them.

CHARLOTTE. It's fine, they're light.

*She walks over to a small table that has a bunch of wild flowers resting on it, and a vase of water. She starts to work on the flowers, cutting off the rougher bits, and the leaves, before inserting them one by one into the vase.*

THEO *places the chairs down.*

THEO. Why did you invite them?

CHARLOTTE. I thought it would be fun.

THEO. Liar.

CHARLOTTE. They're interesting.

THEO. He inveigled himself. You were an easy target. (*Puts on an exaggerated American accent.*) 'I knew you were an actress, Charlotte. You have that thing. Like a kind of restlessness. Are you restless, Charlotte? Are you a searcher?'

CHARLOTTE. He's strange.

THEO. 'What are you searching for, Charlotte?'

CHARLOTTE. My flip-flops, usually.

*He walks up to her, drags her playfully away from the flowers, they embrace.*

They won't stay long.

THEO. The duration of their stay is entirely up to us. We have to be rude, make them feel unwanted and unloved.

CHARLOTTE. You've had a good day.

THEO. Another good day, yes.

CHARLOTTE. Tell me.

THEO. Seven pages. Strong ones, though. I haven't torn them up.

CHARLOTTE. It's flowing.

THEO. Maybe not quite flowing. But trickling with a little more ease than it does in Camberwell.

CHARLOTTE. It's this place. This magical place.

*They kiss.*

HARVEY *and* JUNE *walk on to the terrace but* CHARLOTTE *and* THEO *do not see them; they are still kissing.* HARVEY *and* JUNE *are both dressed quite smartly but there is nothing stuffy about them –* HARVEY *has a loose, somewhat preppy style, and* JUNE *is elegant in an American way. They are a good-looking couple.*

HARVEY. Okay, that's not good, we need to start again.

CHARLOTTE. Hello!

HARVEY. We need to cough, or something. Coughing is always effective, a little clearing of the throat. It's the oldest trick in the book because it works! June, come with me.

*He takes* JUNE *by the hand and leads her off the terrace again, out of sight.*

JUNE. Oh, Harvey, please! Why can't we just make a normal appearance for once?

*Out of sight he starts coughing very loudly, in an exaggerated fashion, almost as if he is choking. Then they reappear and* JUNE *is laughing.*

Now you sound like you're contagious!

THEO. Or consumptive, or something.

HARVEY. You're in love!

JUNE. My God, this view!

HARVEY. I can tell, they're in love! They were kissing, June.

JUNE. I know, I saw them, they were.

THEO. Hello, Harvey.

HARVEY. I know what you're thinking. The Americans. Were you not having that conversation just before we emerged from the bushes?

*THEO and CHARLOTTE are flummoxed; they think they may have been overheard.*

THEO. No, we weren't, I wasn't…

HARVEY. Were you not saying – (*Puts on an exaggerated English accent.*) 'What were you thinking, darling, when you invited those blasted Americans? That man is an aberration.'

THEO. No, I promise, nothing like that.

HARVEY. I believe you, Theo.

CHARLOTTE. We're very happy you're here.

HARVEY. We'll grow on you. You'll see, we do that, don't we, June.

JUNE. He does. He grows on you.

*There is a small pause.*

HARVEY. Where is it?

THEO. Where's what?

HARVEY. Where do you write, Theo? I want to see where you write your plays.

THEO. Well, it varies. I don't really…

HARVEY *walks up to the table with the Corona on it.*

HARVEY. Is this it? This is it, isn't it? Oh my God, here it is.

THEO. There it is.

HARVEY *touches the typewriter.*

HARVEY. The evidence. June, this is it. This is where the man writes.

JUNE. It's a beautiful spot, Theo.

CHARLOTTE. It's his private little table.

HARVEY. With a view to the west. He sits here, on the very edge of the European Continent, a messenger and a guard, both at once. Staring out over the wine-dark sea and writing from the very depth of his soul. Sophocles, Euripides and Theodore…?

THEO. Manning.

HARVEY. This is the only place for you to write, Theodore Manning.

CHARLOTTE. He has been having a creative time, haven't you?

THEO. It's been fine.

*And* HARVEY *now sees the manuscript.*

HARVEY. Oh my dear Lord. And this… can I? May I? Can I?

THEO. I'd rather you didn't. I'm a little…

HARVEY. Superstitious. Of course you are, and you have every right to be. You are communing with the gods, my friend, make sure those sullied, mortal hands stay firmly tucked away.

*He puts his hands in his pockets, like an admonished boy.*

JUNE. He envies you.

HARVEY. I don't envy him, June, I admire him.

JUNE. The two often go together.

HARVEY. How can you not admire a man who does this for a living?

THEO. Tries to.

HARVEY. Even more worthy of my admiration. *Tries* to. Sweats it out. Excavates. Digs with his bare soul to make life a little more bearable for the rest of us even though he can hardly pay the bills.

CHARLOTTE. That last part is true.

THEO. You're getting carried away.

JUNE. He does that.

HARVEY. No, I'm not. And I know you're good.

THEO. How do you know?

HARVEY. I just know these things. You're both good. A fine playwright and a fine actress.

CHARLOTTE. Why are you flattering us, Harvey?

HARVEY. I'm not, Charlotte. That's my gift. Sniffing people out. Identifying. It's what I'm good at.

JUNE. He means it.

HARVEY. I do.

JUNE. After you left us on the port he said to me, 'Those two are talented. You can sense it. They have it.'

THEO. 'It'?

> THEO *and* CHARLOTTE *feel awkward.* CHARLOTTE *breaks the moment with a clap of her hands.*

CHARLOTTE. What shall I get us to drink?

JUNE. Oh, thank God, I thought you'd never ask.

THEO. I'll get them.

CHARLOTTE. We're very low on provisions, I'm afraid, and didn't have a chance to get the bus into the village.

JUNE. And we've come empty-handed.

HARVEY. Siesta time. The shops were all closed. Or should I say, *the* shop.

CHARLOTTE. There's whisky. And something Greek.

JUNE. Something Greek sounds good.

HARVEY. I'll come with you.

THEO. Darling?

CHARLOTTE. A very small whisky.

> THEO *heads off, with* HARVEY *in tow.*

HARVEY. They gave the world civilisation, now they sleep all afternoon.

THEO. They've earned it, I suppose.

*They go.* JUNE *is hovering by the table with the flowers, and notices them.*

JUNE. They're beautiful.

CHARLOTTE. From the garden. I was just arranging them when you arrived…

JUNE. Let's finish the job together.

CHARLOTTE *joins* JUNE *at the table and together they continue pulling the leaves off the flowers and arranging them in the vase.*

It's very kind of you to ask us over.

CHARLOTTE. We wanted to. It's been… we've been living in some isolation.

JUNE. That's romantic.

CHARLOTTE. I've been reading paperback novels and Theo's been writing his play.

JUNE. What's it about?

CHARLOTTE. Oh, he never tells me. But we've been spending so much time on our own so it's nice to talk to people.

JUNE. We forced ourselves onto you.

CHARLOTTE. You did no such thing.

JUNE. Well, Harvey did. It's what he does. He spots people he likes and then he goes for them like a torpedo.

CHARLOTTE. How can he like someone without knowing them?

JUNE. Well, appearances, you know. He liked how you were dressed and we saw the book you were reading, Truman Capote.

CHARLOTTE. Oh, that.

JUNE. And then we overheard some of the conversation you were having.

CHARLOTTE. You did?

JUNE. Oh, that sounds creepy. But you were sitting two tables away, we couldn't help it. You were talking about the theatre –

CHARLOTTE. I was talking about a friend of ours who's performing in a play in the West End, yes.

JUNE. Well, Harvey's *obsessed* with the theatre. When we're in London or New York, he drags me to everything. So he leaned forward and said to me, 'They're my kind of people.'

CHARLOTTE. Then he turned around and introduced himself.

JUNE. Yes.

CHARLOTTE. Well, it's lovely to meet you.

*A pause.*

JUNE. And it's part of his job, really.

CHARLOTTE. What is?

JUNE. Being able to make quick decisions about people, that sort of thing.

CHARLOTTE. I don't think he mentioned what his job is.

JUNE. Oh, Harvey works for the Government. The US Government, I mean.

CHARLOTTE. Of course.

JUNE. He's like a diplomat.

CHARLOTTE. 'Like'?

JUNE. Well, it's complicated. He works for the State Department. He's a floater.

CHARLOTTE. What's a floater?

JUNE. No, I mean, we travel. He gets around. My God, Charlotte, the places I've lived in.

CHARLOTTE. That's exciting, to see the world.

JUNE. I married him when we were both quite young. He'd just left Harvard, I was modelling in New York. Six months later, we're in Persia and I'm curtsying in front of the Shah.

CHARLOTTE. How glamorous.

JUNE. Sometimes it is. But I miss having a base, a home. We do have a little brownstone in Washington but we're hardly ever there.

CHARLOTTE. And you've been living in Athens?

JUNE. For the last few months, yes.

CHARLOTTE. Have you enjoyed it?

JUNE. It's okay. Harvey's always busy so I try to find my own things.

CHARLOTTE. What sort of things?

JUNE. Depends where we're at. So in Athens, for instance, I thought I'd learn something about the ancient history, that sort of thing. So I was taking a course at the American College. And then there's the embassy people too, cocktail parties, barbecues, you know.

CHARLOTTE. Of course.

JUNE. Sometimes it gets lonely but I can't complain.

*Pause. They have finished with the flowers, and* JUNE *moves away from the table.*

But we're moving back soon, things are coming to a close.

CHARLOTTE. What things?

JUNE. I'm not mad about Athens but the islands are divine. Not the arid ones to the south but these northern ones are beautiful and green.

CHARLOTTE. So you're here for a short holiday?

JUNE. Harvey said we should get out of Athens for a few days. His job is nearly done, and things are heating up a little.

THEO *and* HARVEY *come out of the house. They are holding two glasses each.*

HARVEY. What's heating up? You're not talking politics again, are you?

THEO *gives one to* CHARLOTTE, HARVEY *gives one to* JUNE.

CHARLOTTE. Thank you, darling.

JUNE. Would I ever?

HARVEY. Don't bore Charlotte with the boring stuff.

CHARLOTTE. So, darling, June was saying that Harvey works for the Government.

THEO. Oh, right.

HARVEY. That's what I mean by the boring stuff.

CHARLOTTE. June said you were a floater, Harvey.

JUNE. Geographically, I meant, not in any other way.

CHARLOTTE. Not ideologically, or anything.

JUNE. No, I meant, as in we travel a lot.

HARVEY. We do, we do, we do.

THEO. How wonderful for you.

*Pause.* HARVEY *decides to change the subject and he does it with a burst of new energy.*

HARVEY. So what's the play about? I will not touch it with my grubby claws but give me something, for God's sake.

JUNE. He doesn't say, Harvey, so don't push him.

HARVEY. Not a word, not a syllable?

CHARLOTTE. No, not a word.

HARVEY. Not a crumb? I don't know, something like, 'pain'. Or 'innocence', or, maybe, if you're feeling generous 'my mother's fondness for gin' or 'the day Uncle Desmond rubbed up against me for just a minute too long'.

JUNE. Harvey Parker.

HARVEY. What was the inception? The trigger?

CHARLOTTE. He really doesn't like telling people.

THEO. I just don't talk about it. When I'm working on it, I mean. And I don't think it's superstitious. It's something else. I'm nervous of...

HARVEY. Dissipation.

THEO. Well, yes, I suppose...

HARVEY. And so you should. It's sacred. Keep it close, Theo.

THEO. I'll try.

HARVEY. But the most important thing is, you have been working. The *only* important thing. The Muse is sitting here, on this terrace. We can not see her, but her presence is felt.

JUNE. I feel her, I feel her!

THEO. She was having a siesta this afternoon, along with everyone else, but the morning was good.

HARVEY. And tomorrow she will be with you again.

THEO. Here's hoping.

HARVEY. To the Muse!

*They toast –* HARVEY *and* JUNE *with enthusiasm,* THEO *and* CHARLOTTE *with slight bemusement.*

Because you see, Theo, Charlotte – I love the theatre.

CHARLOTTE. June said.

HARVEY. No, I mean, I *love* the theatre. I love all art – well, most art – but more than any other art form I love the theatre. Do you know why I love the theatre?

THEO. Why do you love the theatre, Harvey?

HARVEY. I love the theatre because she's democracy's twin.

JUNE. And Harvey loves democracy.

HARVEY. They were born together, were they not?

THEO. They were indeed.

HARVEY. Just, what – less than one hundred miles away from here, and together they came spitting and crying into this savage world and together they crawled, and together they learnt to walk, and talk, and gave us everything we hold dear.

THEO. He likes the theatre.

HARVEY. But I mean seriously, have you thought of that? How they both just, *emerged*, just morphed into being, at pretty much exactly the same time? That the two of them just appeared simultaneously? Have you thought of that?

THEO. Just a little.

JUNE. I told you he's passionate about it.

HARVEY. People in a space telling other people a story and then asking them, 'What would you do, little man? What would you do if you were in my place? What would you do if you found out you'd been fucking your mother'…

JUNE. Language, Harvey!

THEO. It's the passion talking.

HARVEY. Or some knuckle-head leader barred you from burying your own brother in the rightful way or God knows what, what would you do, little man? Because that's what theatre is, *was*, and the Greeks knew that – that's what *tragedy* is, that point, after the debate, when the audience, have to make a choice. And that choice will make a difference to the state, you know, the *demos*, the community, whatever, the way they all live.

THEO. Wow.

*They think it's over. And he's off again.*

HARVEY. And the playwright – and Theo, you know what the playwright, what *you*, are called, what the word in Greek is?

THEO. *Didaskalos?*

HARVEY. Thank you, which means…

THEO. Teacher?

HARVEY. Someone who shows you the way, takes you by the hand and leads you to a place where you might have a broader perspective of yourself and the world you live in.

THEO. I'd be a little nervous to describe myself in that particular way.

CHARLOTTE. Theo's modest.

HARVEY. But the point being that these guys – these *didaskaloi*, these teachers, whatever you want to call them, were part of the system. They were questioning things, they were making people uncomfortable, they were rocking the boat – but they were doing it from *within*. Christ, Sophocles was made a general, Aeschylus fought the Persians at Marathon, they were part of the world they were interrogating, they were shaking it from inside, but they were *loyal to it*.

THEO. Loyal.

HARVEY. You and I need each other, Theo, we're a pair. Bread and butter, whisky and soda.

THEO. Cheese and pickle.

HARVEY. Stay loyal, Theo, stay loyal.

THEO. I'll do my best.

JUNE. Sweetheart, take a break. You need to breathe.

*Suddenly,* MARIA *and* STAMATIS *appear from the pathway. They are local Greeks, simply dressed. They edge their way forward tentatively.* MARIA *speaks English with quite a heavy Greek accent.*

MARIA. *Yia sas.*

CHARLOTTE. Hello.

HARVEY. Enter the Greeks.

MARIA. Good evening. It is Friday.

CHARLOTTE. Friday, yes.

MARIA. We have come for the taking of the furniture.

CHARLOTTE. The furniture?

*Suddenly,* CHARLOTTE *remembers.*

Good God, yes, of course, I'm so sorry.

HARVEY. They're taking your furniture?

CHARLOTTE. I'm so sorry, I completely forgot. Darling, it's Friday.

THEO. Friday, yes?

CHARLOTTE. Do you remember, I told you that Maria and her father were coming by to pick up that furniture from the basement?

THEO. Of course.

CHARLOTTE. Maria, this is, these are our friends.

JUNE. Hi, Maria.

CHARLOTTE. This is Maria, everyone, and her father, Mr… Mr…

MARIA. Mr Stamatis, he does not speak English.

STAMATIS *bows his head in greeting.*

HARVEY. But you do it for the both of you, and you do it well.

CHARLOTTE. Maria and her family are the owners of this beautiful house, we are renting it from them.

HARVEY. Maria, you've been uprooted.

CHARLOTTE. Maria and her family are about to move. I mean more than move…

THEO. They're emigrating.

MARIA. To Australia, yes. To the Sydney.

HARVEY. The Sydney. How exciting.

CHARLOTTE. They've kindly moved out of the house while we're here…

HARVEY. Kindness has nothing to do with it, Charlotte, it's economic necessity.

MARIA. We are staying with my uncle in the village.

CHARLOTTE. And they're here to pick up some furniture of theirs from the basement.

MARIA. We will try and sell it.

HARVEY. Of course.

CHARLOTTE. Well, you know the way in. And do let us know, if there's anything you need, we're more than happy to help.

MARIA. Thank you, Mrs Manning.

*She turns to her father.*

*Έλα Πατέρα.* [Come on, Father.]

*They enter the house.*

JUNE. What a lovely girl.

CHARLOTTE. She's a darling, yes.

JUNE. Have you met the whole family?

CHARLOTTE. I get the feeling it's just the two of them.

THEO. No sign of the mother.

JUNE. And how did you find them and their beautiful house?

THEO. Plain good luck.

CHARLOTTE. Yes, luck really. We came to the island blindly, we'd been told we would easily find somewhere to stay, especially since it's this time of year.

JUNE. Off season.

CHARLOTTE. But we were expecting a room, or something, you know, a bed and breakfast.

HARVEY. And then you found Maria.

THEO. We asked in the port, that little tobacconist place near where you step off the ferry and the man happened to be Maria's uncle, the father's brother.

CHARLOTTE. Next thing you know we were being driven here in one of those things, the open cars with three wheels. We were like a couple of goats.

THEO. We arrived here and we fell in love.

HARVEY. How lucky.

*Slight pause.*

JUNE. Can I? Is there any more of this Greek stuff?

CHARLOTTE. Of course, I'm so sorry, I'll fetch the bottle.

THEO. We thought you'd like it.

JUNE. It works.

CHARLOTTE. And I'll fetch the whisky, too.

JUNE. Can I take a peek? At the house, I mean. Can I look inside? I'm so curious.

CHARLOTTE. Of course you can, it's lovely. Come with me, I'll give you the tour.

*The women enter the house.* HARVEY *watches them go, and the men are left alone.*

HARVEY. She protects you.

*He starts to wander around the space, taking it all in, but he gravitates back towards the table with the typewriter and the manuscript on it.*

Okay, Theo, so humour me, will you.

THEO. I'll do my best.

HARVEY. So I understand that you'd rather not talk about what it is you're writing.

THEO. Correct.

HARVEY. But could you talk to me about the process a little. I mean what it's like. What it *feels* like. To sit down at this place and create stories, debates, myths, whatever it is you create. What does that feel like, Theo?

*Pause.*

It's all I ask.

*Pause.* THEO *thinks for a little.*

THEO. Okay, I'll try.

*He thinks a little more.*

You have a sketch, maybe. Well, I mean I do. A plan. And something you feel you want to explore.

HARVEY. A road map and a terrain.

THEO. And then you set off into – yes, into this *terrain*, I suppose – and then you realise that the road map is not quite accurate. But as you come to realise that you also start to think that perhaps it's not even necessary. What I mean is...

HARVEY. That once you're in the terrain, the road map becomes a little redundant?

THEO. But you needed it to begin with. Maybe just for confidence, I don't know. And then this other thing takes over, and it's the intelligence, I don't know...

HARVEY. Of the terrain itself, Theo. The intelligence of the world.

THEO. Something like that.

*Pause.*

HARVEY. Maybe June's right. Maybe I am a little envious of you. Because I don't have access to that intelligence. I only have my own.

THEO. Your own?

HARVEY. My own intelligence, I mean. It's all I have.

*Pause.*

And do you know, I think I'm falling a little in love with you.

*Pause.*

Oh, don't get nervous, I'm not a pansy, I'm not a queer. I don't want to mount you.

THEO. That's a relief.

HARVEY. I'm just falling a little in love with you, is all.

*Pause.*

These are exciting times to be alive, aren't they?

THEO. Are there ever dull ones?

HARVEY. Change, I mean. It's everywhere. In the air, and on the ground and in the smell of my wife's hair.

THEO. What sort of change?

HARVEY. Those girls – I mean Charlotte and June. The world is opening for them. In the next ten years, things are going to change for them. It's going to be different. I think of my mother, you know, corseted into submission, a forced silence – and then I see June, and I'm excited for her. Because the opportunities – you know, for self-expression, for freedom, that sort of thing.

THEO. Yes.

HARVEY. And other things, too. I mean in the States, in my country, major things are happening to the coloured community. Civil rights, and now, a constant effort to question what the role of that race is within the society, and we are allowing them, the *system* is allowing them to forge their way forward and ask those all-important questions.

THEO. Allowing them?

HARVEY. So that they too can play their part in this great democracy.

THEO. I see.

HARVEY. So it's an exciting time to be alive. And especially to be a *didaskalos*.

*Pause.*

THEO. It's funny.

HARVEY. What is, Theo?

THEO. It's just a coincidence, that's all.

HARVEY. Because you happen to be writing something about coloured people?

THEO. Good God, no, I wouldn't dare. I mean, it's not quite within my sphere of experience.

HARVEY. But you're writing something similar?

THEO. Well, I mean, not really, but it's a coincidence.

HARVEY. Is it?

*Pause.*

THEO. A very dear friend of mine was arrested for, what they call in England, importuning, for, it's like… indecent…

HARVEY. He's a queer.

THEO. Well, in a word, yes. And he is the nicest man, and a good friend, intelligent, a profound thinker…

HARVEY. Why shouldn't he be?

THEO. And he has no way of meeting other people, and there is much hatred aimed towards him, and it feels unjust, and it needs to be…

HARVEY. Explored. Interrogated. Put in front of an audience.

THEO. Well, yes. I suppose.

HARVEY. You're right, it does, I agree.

*Pause. When* HARVEY *speaks it is genuine, with affection, and sincerity. But he touches the manuscript gently with his hand.*

Thank you for telling me.

*And only then does* THEO *realise what he's done.*

*There is a commotion and* CHARLOTTE, JUNE, MARIA *and* STAMATIS *emerge from the house, all of them carrying a large chest of drawers.*

JUNE. Look what we found, Harvey.

HARVEY. Jesus.

JUNE. Isn't it wonderful?

CHARLOTTE. It's quite heavy, we had to give them a hand.

*They put it down; rest.*

MARIA. Thank you very much.

CHARLOTTE. Leave it here for the minute and once you've got the chairs and the sideboard we can carry them all down the path to the driveway. Then the truck can pick it all up from there.

JUNE. Isn't it gorgeous, Harvey? It's from the 1920s. Made by a man in the village, the carpenter. It has this beautiful design on the surface, come see.

CHARLOTTE. Oh, the drinks!

*CHARLOTTE runs back into the house.*

*HARVEY and THEO both approach the chest of drawers. They all congregate around it, start to explore it, opening drawers, running their hands across the surface of it, admiring it.*

HARVEY. Oh, that's pretty, what is it? Are those goats?

JUNE. It's like a pastoral thing, you know a pastoral scene or whatever you want to call it, all done with such detail and care. Look at those little things, like little cottages, aren't they adorable?

THEO. They look like this one.

MARIA. It was the property of my grandmother.

JUNE. Well, your grandmother had great taste, Maria.

*CHARLOTTE returns with a tray. On it are two bottles – the whisky and the Greek stuff. She rests it somewhere, then picks up the bottles and goes around refreshing the glasses that people are holding. The whisky bottle is nearly empty.*

*JUNE opens one of the drawers.*

And look, Harvey, it's deceptive. So much space in those drawers. So it's practical, too.

HARVEY. Yes, very.

JUNE. Isn't it just divine, Harvey?

HARVEY. It is, June, it is.

JUNE. It's beautiful and practical, both at once.

HARVEY. But I'm not having it shipped to Washington, sweetheart, so you can forget it.

JUNE. Killjoy.

THEO. It's a very special piece of furniture, Maria.

MARIA. Thank you.

HARVEY. And now you have to sell it.

MARIA. We will try.

JUNE. That's sad.

HARVEY. You need money for the move to Australia, right?

MARIA. We have already the tickets, but yes, we need more money.

HARVEY. So you're all set to sail?

MARIA. In two weeks we take the boat from Piraeus.

HARVEY. That's a long journey.

MARIA. Yes, very.

HARVEY. I wish you nothing but the best.

*Pause. He runs his hand across the surface of the chest of drawers.*

And what about the house?

MARIA. The house?

HARVEY. Are you selling the house as well?

JUNE. Why are you asking, Harvey?

HARVEY. I just want to know, that's all.

MARIA. The house?

JUNE. But why?

HARVEY. Yes. Are you selling the house?

*There is a pause.* STAMATIS *speaks in Greek.*

STAMATIS. *Τι λέει;* [What's he saying?]

MARIA. *Ρωτάει άμα πουλάμε το σπίτι.* [He's asking if we're selling the house.]

STAMATIS. *Το σπίτι;* [The house?]

MARIA. *Ναι, ρωτάει άμα το πουλάμε.* [Yes, he's asking if we're selling the house.]

HARVEY. Well, are you?

THEO. Why do you want to know if they're selling the house, Harvey?

HARVEY. I'm just asking. Can't a man ask a question without being pounced on?

STAMATIS. *Γιατί ρωτάει άμα πουλάμε το σπίτι;* [Why is he asking if we want to sell the house?]

MARIA. *Δεν ξέρω πατέρα.* [I don't know, Dad.]

STAMATIS. *Θέλει να το αγοράσει;* [Does he want to buy it?]

MARIA. He is asking do you want to buy it?

HARVEY. Well, I'm just asking, but yes, well, maybe, yes, maybe we do want to buy it. But I'm just asking.

JUNE. Harvey, where are you going with this?

CHARLOTTE. We? Who's we?

HARVEY. Depending of course on what kind of arrangement we can come to.

THEO. He means we as in 'me and June', darling.

CHARLOTTE. I hope so.

HARVEY. But I'm open to negotiation. And you can throw the furniture in, saves you from carrying it down that path.

STAMATIS. *Τι λέει;* [What's he saying?]

HARVEY. Maria, let's not get carried away. Why don't you and your dad continue with what you were doing and then, depending on how things evolve here between the four of us, we can resume the conversation?

MARIA *seems a little confused.*

MARIA. I don't understand.

HARVEY. I mean just carry on with what you were doing.

MARIA. Yes.

*She turns to* STAMATIS.

*Έλα πατέρα, πάμε να μαζέψουμε τις καρέκλες.* [Come, Dad, let's go get the chairs.]

MARIA *leads a bemused* STAMATIS *back into the house.*

HARVEY. Hello, can I speak to Theodore Manning, please?

THEO. Speaking.

HARVEY. Theo Manning, this is your Destiny calling.

CHARLOTTE. I knew it.

THEO. Hello, Destiny?

HARVEY. Okay, so now, listen, I need you both to listen to me, and listen to me carefully –

JUNE. What are you doing, Harvey?

CHARLOTTE. I think I know what he's doing.

HARVEY. And I'm feeling the resistance already, Charlotte, but you really need to listen to me because this is important, maybe the most important moment of your lives.

THEO. We're listening.

CHARLOTTE. Oh, for God's sake.

HARVEY. Because, Charlotte, when I saw you here, when
I walked onto this terrace earlier this evening and saw you
kissing your husband the playwright right here on this spot,
I *knew* this was your house.

THEO. Our house?

HARVEY. And maybe now you have to also entertain the notion
that I too have come into your lives for a particular reason.

*He walks up to the table with the typewriter and manuscript
on it. He goes full throttle, giving a performance.*

Because it is here, my friend, at this table, with this glorious
view of the sea that you will write your greatest plays. And
write a part for Charlotte, too, the kind of part she deserves,
and yearns for, am I right, Charlotte?

CHARLOTTE. That's cheap.

HARVEY. Maybe it's cheap, yes, I'm working hard, too hard,
but it's true, Charlotte, he will, and you want that, don't you,
so he *will*, and as he writes it your children will be playing at
your feet and you will walk them down to the beach every
morning and swim in that blessed sea. This is your house,
Theo, Charlotte. I knew it from the moment I saw you here.
This is your house, the house of your dreams.

CHARLOTTE. And why do you care so much?

HARVEY. You really want to know?

CHARLOTTE. Yes, I do, I want to know.

THEO. Why are you so keen for us to buy it, Harvey?

CHARLOTTE. Yes, why?

HARVEY. BECAUSE I WANT YOU TO BE HAPPY!

*Pause.*

THEO. He's persuasive, isn't he?

JUNE. I married the man.

CHARLOTTE. But it's ridiculous.

HARVEY. Why is it ridiculous?

CHARLOTTE. Because even if we did, I mean even if we loved the house…

HARVEY. You do love the house, Charlotte, that part's not hypothetical.

CHARLOTTE. But even if we do, we could never buy it.

HARVEY. Why not?

CHARLOTTE. Because we can't afford it.

HARVEY. Yes, you can, you can afford it.

THEO. How can we afford it?

HARVEY. You can afford it because it's very, very cheap.

*Pause.*

Maria and her family are moving to Australia.

THEO. I know that.

HARVEY. You know why they're moving to Australia?

CHARLOTTE. Because they need to.

HARVEY. Yes, that's right, because they need to, they desperately need to.

JUNE. I hope Maria succeeds, she's a nice girl.

HARVEY. So do I, June, so do I. But the point is that in order to begin this new life and give his daughter the opportunities she deserves, her father is having to sell their furniture. That is how much they need the money. My suspicion is that the only reason he hasn't put the house on the market – apart from sentimental reasons – is that he hasn't thought anyone would want to buy it. Most people are not like you, they don't appreciate, how shall I put it, rustic peasant dwellings, and property's not moving here anyway, it's undiscovered.

THEO. So what you're saying is…

HARVEY. What I'm saying is that Maria and her father need the money so bad that they'll sell you the house of your dreams for close to nothing.

*Pause.*

CHARLOTTE. But that's immoral.

HARVEY. Why is it immoral, Charlotte?

CHARLOTTE. It's exploitative.

HARVEY. Why?

CHARLOTTE. Because you are taking advantage of the fact that they are in need, that they are down.

HARVEY. So give them triple what they ask for, Charlotte. If you have the money and you really care for them, give them triple what they ask for.

*Pause.*

THEO. How much do you think…

CHARLOTTE. Theo!

HARVEY. I don't know, all we have to do is ask. I mean if it's crazy, well, then obviously, it's a non-starter and this conversation is a waste of time. But if it's the price of a jar of peanut butter, which I suspect it may well be, you'd be foolish not to consider it. You love this place.

THEO. It's true, but…

CHARLOTTE. Theo, can I talk to you?

HARVEY. Of course.

CHARLOTTE. Oh, thank you, Harvey, but I mean in private.

HARVEY. So June and I will take our drinks and stroll for a short while down in those pine trees and we will join you again presently. Come on, sweetheart.

*He leads the way.*

JUNE. Sometimes you really go too far, Harvey Parker.

*They go; CHARLOTTE and THEO are left alone.*
*CHARLOTTE starts pacing.*

CHARLOTTE. Theo, what are you doing?

THEO. What am I doing, I haven't done anything.

CHARLOTTE. How can you even be serious about it? We've only just met him.

THEO. It's not about him, it's about the house.

CHARLOTTE. But he's directing it all.

THEO. But what if he wasn't here? I mean, what if we had the idea ourselves? Does it matter that it's come from him?

*She checks to see she's not being overheard.*

CHARLOTTE. I don't like him.

THEO. Why not?

CHARLOTTE. Why is he deciding things for us? And then talking to that poor girl about it, on our behalf? As if he owns us all.

THEO. I don't see it like that.

CHARLOTTE. And then saying, 'Buy it while it's cheap. Rob them in broad daylight.' I mean this house has probably been theirs for generations.

THEO. But he's also right when he says we might be doing them a favour. That we'll be helping them, Charlotte, that we'll be giving them a helping hand.

CHARLOTTE. Oh, Theo, don't be so naive.

THEO. Anyway, for just one moment let's keep him out of the equation. Just for a minute, Charlotte, let's keep him out.

*Pause.*

I do love it here, Charlotte. I've never written like this, it's true. He's right.

CHARLOTTE. I thought you said we'd keep him out of the equation.

THEO. We knew it from the first minute we got here. That first evening, do you remember? We sat here, the two of us, looking at that sunset and do you remember what we said to each other?

CHARLOTTE. That we'd never been to such a beautiful place.

THEO. And we do have that money from my aunt which we've put aside. I mean it may not be enough but…

CHARLOTTE. That money's for when we have children, Theo, we said we wouldn't touch it.

THEO. Well, this place would be for our children too. And I think we could be so happy. And we could rent it out on the side. I mean if things got tough. It's cheap to run and our summers would be… our summers would be blissful, Charlotte.

CHARLOTTE. I know.

THEO. So all I'm saying is let's consider it, that's all.

*Pause.*

And I don't think he's that bad. I mean he's full of himself, and yes, a bit of a bully, and bullish and all those things but he's also charming and there's something else…

*He thinks for a minute as if trying to come up with the right word but then gives up.*

It's more complicated is what I mean. But anyway, we're getting carried away. They probably don't even want to sell the place.

MARIA *emerges from the house with* STAMATIS *in tow. They approach* CHARLOTTE *and* THEO *a little sheepishly.*

MARIA. Mrs Manning, Mr Manning.

CHARLOTTE. Hello, Maria.

STAMATIS. *Πες τους, μίλα τους.* [Tell them, talk to them.]

MARIA. My father wants me to speak with you and with also the American man.

THEO. He's gone for a little walk, you can tell us, Maria.

STAMATIS. *Που είναι ο Αμερικάνος;* [Where is the American?]

MARIA. *Λένε να μιλήσουμε μ' αυτούς.* [They say we can talk to them.]

STAMATIS. *Πες τους ό,τι είπα, όπως τα είπα.* [Tell them exactly what I said, the way I said it.]

THEO. What is it, Maria? What do you want to tell us?

*MARIA starts to speak but she is finding it hard to conceal her emotion and her voice quivers with it a little.*

MARIA. My father wants me to say to you that we will be very happy if the man will buy the house.

THEO. It's not for him, Maria, it's for us, we're the ones who might be interested in buying the house. Who are considering it, I mean.

STAMATIS. *Εκατό σαράντα χιλιάδες, αλλά σε Αυστραλέζικα δολάρια, όπως είπαμε.* [One hundred and forty thousand, but in Australian dollars, like we said.]

MARIA. The cost will be one hundred and forty thousand drachmas.

THEO. One hundred and forty?

MARIA. But my father is saying that you must pay all the monies in the bank in Australia.

THEO. In Australian dollars, yes, of course, that makes sense, that wouldn't be difficult.

STAMATIS. *Τι λέει;* [What's he saying?]

THEO *turns to* CHARLOTTE.

THEO. One hundred and forty thousand, eighty-three drachmas to the pound, that's under one thousand seven hundred pounds.

CHARLOTTE. That can't be right.

STAMATIS. *Να τα βάλουμε στο λογαριασμό στο Sydney.*
[They put it in a bank in Sydney.]

MARIA. My father says you place the monies in the bank in
the Sydney.

CHARLOTTE. The thing is, Maria, we're not really sure that…

STAMATIS. *Και πες τους για τα στρέμματα.* [And tell them
about the acres.]

MARIA. *Δεν ξέρω πως λέγονται τα στρέμματα στα
Αγγλικά.* [I don't know what the word for acres is.]

STAMATIS. *Τότε πες τους για το κτήμα. Τι θα πάρουν με
τα λεφτά τους!* [Tell them about the land then. What they
get for their money!]

CHARLOTTE. I mean it's a big decision, Maria, and we need a
little time to think. That man, the American I mean, was
being a little hasty.

STAMATIS. *Πες τους για το κτήμα, πες τους για τα
δέντρα!* [Tell them about the land, tell them about the trees!]

THEO. That's less than half of my aunt's money, Charlotte.

CHARLOTTE. And Mr Manning and I are not rich people,
you understand.

STAMATIS. *Πες τους, Πες τους!* [Tell them, tell them!]

MARIA. My father is wanting me also to tell you that with it
comes the trees.

THEO. Trees, what trees?

CHARLOTTE. The pine forest.

STAMATIS. *Τα δέντρα, τους είπες για τα δέντρα;* [The
trees, did you tell them about the trees?]

MARIA. *Ναι πατέρα, ναι πατέρα, τους το'πα!* [Yes, Dad,
yes, Dad, I told them!]

THEO. So you mean there's land, Maria, that comes with the
house?

CHARLOTTE. That's what she's saying, Theo.

THEO. And what's the land, Maria? I mean where does it start and where does it end?

STAMATIS (*increasingly forceful*). *Και για την παραλία! Ψυχή δεν πατάει! Σαν ιδιωτική παραλία είναι, πες τους το!* [And the beach! No one ever comes to that beach! It's like a private beach, tell them!]

MARIA. And the beach!

THEO. What beach?

CHARLOTTE. Theo!

STAMATIS. *Πες τους το! Για όνομα του Θεού, πες τους το!* [Tell them! For God's sake, tell them!]

MARIA. The house, and the trees, and the sea!

*And she suddenly bursts into tears.*

STAMATIS. *Τρελάθηκες; Τι έβαλες τα κλάματα;* [Have you lost your mind? What are you crying for?]

MARIA. *Το δάσος πατέρα, το δάσος!* [The forest, Dad, the forest.]

CHARLOTTE. Maria, what's wrong?

THEO. God.

CHARLOTTE. Why are you so upset, we don't want to upset you.

STAMATIS (*screaming at the top of his voice now*). *Για συμμαζέψου λιγάκι! Για σένα τα᾿ χουμε ανάγκη τα χρήματα!* [Pull yourself together! It's you we need the money for!]

MARIA (*through tears*). *Είναι το σπίτι της γιαγιάς πατέρα, είναι το σπίτι της γιαγιάς!* [It's Yia-yia's house, Dad, it's Yia-yia's house.]

STAMATIS. *Το σπίτι δικό μας είναι και τα λεφτά τα᾿ χουμε ανάγκη!* [The house is ours and we need the money!]

THEO. You really don't need to shout at her, we don't want to upset anyone.

CHARLOTTE. What's happening, Maria? Why are you so upset?

STAMATIS. *Θα με τρελάνεις!* [You'll drive me crazy!]

*But* MARIA *keeps crying.* HARVEY *and* JUNE *return, glasses in hand.*

HARVEY. Decision time. Have you chosen hope or fear?

*They notice* MARIA.

Dear Lord, what have you done to her?

THEO. We haven't done a thing, I promise.

STAMATIS (*still shouting at the top of his voice*). *Σταμάτα να κλαίς σαν μωρό και συμμαζέψου!* [Stop crying like a baby and pull yourself together!]

JUNE. Why is he screaming at her?

THEO. Please don't shout at her, it was just a question.

CHARLOTTE. What's wrong, Maria, tell me what's wrong.

JUNE. Don't cry, little girl.

*Still through tears,* MARIA *starts to speak.*

MARIA. It's my yia-yia's house, Mrs Manning, my yia-yia's.

CHARLOTTE. Yia-yia's?

HARVEY. Her grandmother's.

STAMATIS. *Μην μου τα χαλάσεις τώρα, θα σε σφάξω!* [Don't go ruining things now, I'll kill you!]

CHARLOTTE. Oh, I see, of course.

MARIA. When my yia-yia was still living she sit with me here – here, exactly here, where you are standing, Mrs Manning, and she says to me, 'One day, when you are a lady, Maria, this house will be yours, promise me, Maria, you will always look after this house' and now Mrs Manning, we go to Australia, I hope that one day I will be possible to come back to the island, and this house, my yia-yia's house.

CHARLOTTE. Of course, I understand, Maria. But listen to me, you needn't worry, we're not going to take the house away from you, and we won't make you break the promise you made your yia-yia, we'd never do that. So you can stop crying now.

MARIA *pulls herself together, stops crying.* CHARLOTTE *hands her a handkerchief.*

MARIA. Thank you, Mrs Manning.

CHARLOTTE. There's nothing to thank me for.

HARVEY. I go away five minutes and the whole thing falls apart.

CHARLOTTE *and* JUNE *both give him a look.* STAMATIS *suddenly surprises them by speaking in English.*

STAMATIS. One hundred forty thousand!

THEO. That's what they're asking for it.

HARVEY. What did I tell you? Peanut butter.

CHARLOTTE. *He's* asking for it, Theo, she isn't.

THEO. It's his house, darling.

CHARLOTTE. It's theirs.

STAMATIS. One hundred forty!

THEO. In Australian dollars, yes.

HARVEY. I mean, that's like, you know, that's cheap.

CHARLOTTE. We know it's cheap, Harvey, we know that.

STAMATIS. One hundred forty!

THEO. He's very keen to sell it, Charlotte.

HARVEY. He's more than keen, he's going to take a chunk out of your leg.

CHARLOTTE. We can see that.

STAMATIS. One hundred thirty!

THEO. No, no, keep it at one hundred and forty, one hundred and forty is fine, we just need a little time to think about it.

HARVEY. You'd be keen if you were moving to a strange part of the world with close to nothing and had your family to protect.

MARIA (*quietly, almost to herself*). I make promise to my yia-yia.

 HARVEY *suddenly beckons to* MARIA.

HARVEY. Maria, can I talk to you for a short while?

 MARIA *slowly steps forward.* HARVEY *takes her aside but the others can still hear what they're saying. He speaks to her gently, comfortingly.*

 Okay, Maria, listen to me. There's no reason to be upset any more. We don't like to see you upset. So let me tell you what will happen.

CHARLOTTE. How do you know what will happen?

HARVEY. Let me tell you what I *think* will happen, Maria, what I *hope* will happen. But first let me try and understand why you are so upset.

 *Pause.*

 You love this house. You love it because it is full of memories of happy times. And sad ones, too. Sometimes the sad ones mean even more than the happy ones. They go deeper.

CHARLOTTE. God Almighty.

HARVEY (*with a little anger aimed at* CHARLOTTE *in his voice*). They do.

 *Pause.*

 You grew up here.

MARIA. Yes.

HARVEY. And you would run though those trees in the mornings and down to the sea.

MARIA. Yes, with no shoes on.

HARVEY. With no shoes on. And I imagine your yia-yia would cook things here for you, because they do that, don't they? Yia-yias do that.

MARIA. Yes, she was a very good cook.

HARVEY. And she taught you. Did she make fig jam?

CHARLOTTE. Fig jam!

MARIA. Yes, how did you know?

CHARLOTTE. He knows things.

HARVEY. And those little things, those round little potato-cake things.

MARIA. *Πατατοκεφτέδες!* [Patatokeftethes!]

HARVEY. Patatoke… whatever.

*Pause.* MARIA *smiles, she thinks it's amusing that he can't pronounce it.*

So listen to me now, Maria. If your father decides to sell the house – either to Theo and Charlotte, or to anybody else –

MARIA. There is nobody else who will buy the house.

HARVEY. But if he does, you take those memories – of your yia-yia and the pine trees, of the sea and the fig jam and the potato thingies…

JUNE. Patatokeftethes.

HARVEY. And you take those precious memories and you move on. Because I know something else about you, Maria.

CHARLOTTE. Of course you do.

MARIA *throws a quick look at* CHARLOTTE.

HARVEY. Listen to me now, Maria, don't listen to Charlotte.

*She turns back to him. Again his voice goes quieter and he
speaks with a slow-burning intent, and feeling too.*

You speak good English, you've worked hard at it. I like the
way you speak for your father. You represent him, you take
responsibility. Five years from now your English will be very
fine indeed. Read as much as you can in Sydney and always
be curious. Every morning when you wake, set your mind to
the task at hand. Pray – to whoever or whatever you pray to –
for strength and reassurance. Or if you're not the praying kind
then just be focused, that's all you need. Challenge your father
when you do not agree with what he is saying. Don't be
frightened of him, his bark is definitely worse than his bite.

CHARLOTTE. Another risky guess.

HARVEY. And whatever you do, do not be discouraged by
those who want to stop you dreaming and achieving. The
only reason they will try and do so – sometimes to great
effect – is because they haven't found a way of doing it
themselves and they resent you for it.

*Pause.*

So take this place in your heart and move forward. This is a
good time to leave Greece, Maria, your father has made an
intelligent decision. Things are difficult here but in a few
years they will be better again. And one day, you will come
back and buy another house here, and start new memories
for your children and your children's children. Because what
your yia-yia wanted more than anything else, was for you to
be happy, and for her house to be loved. And Theo and
Charlotte will love her house and honour her memory. So
you won't have broken the promise.

CHARLOTTE. Incredible.

*Pause. MARIA thinks a little, then walks up to
CHARLOTTE.*

MARIA. I would like you to have my yia-yia's house, Mrs
Manning. You are a very nice woman and Mr Manning too
he is nice man.

HARVEY. They are.

MARIA. You will look over it, yes?

CHARLOTTE (*not quite believing what she's saying*). Look after it, yes, yes we shall.

MARIA. The garden and the house...

CHARLOTTE. And the pine forest that runs down to the sea, yes.

MARIA. Thank you.

*She leans forward and gives* CHARLOTTE *a small kiss on the cheek. She then starts moving back towards the chest of drawers and her father. But she stops, and turns.*

And you will have the furniture, too, Mrs Manning.

CHARLOTTE. If that's what you want, Maria.

MARIA. For just another ten thousand drachmas.

HARVEY. Good girl.

*And she goes to her father.*

STAMATIS. *Τι έγινε; Θα μου πεις τι στο διάολο έγινε;* [What happened? Will you tell me what the hell has happened?]

MARIA. *Το πουλήσαμε πατέρα. Και τα έπιπλα, για δέκα χιλιάδες.* [We sold it, Dad. And the furniture. For ten thousand.]

STAMATIS. *Δέκα χιλιάδες;* [Ten thousand?]

MARIA. *Ναι. Εκατόν σαράντα χιλιάδες για το σπίτι και δέκα χιλιάδες για τα έπιπλα.* [Yes. One hundred and forty thousand for the house and ten thousand for all the furniture.]

STAMATIS *walks up to her, grabs her head in his hands, and plants a big kiss on her forehead.*

STAMATIS. *Κορίτσι μου, Θησαυρέ μου! Θα προκόψεις!* [My girl, my treasure! You'll go far!]

*He turns to the others.*

Whisky! Whisky!

HARVEY. Yes! Whisky! Definitely whisky!

THEO (*holding up the whisky bottle*). This one is finished.

CHARLOTTE. There's another one in the kitchen.

STAMATIS *runs towards the house.*

STAMATIS. *Έλα Μαρία! Πάμε να βρούμε το Ουίσκι! Να το γλεντήσουμε μαζί τους!* [Come, Maria! Come and find the whisky! We celebrate with them!]

MARIA. He wants us to get the whisky. He wants everyone to have the whisky.

HARVEY. What a fine idea.

THEO. I'll come and show you where it is.

MARIA. It is fine, Mr Manning, I will find it.

CHARLOTTE. It's on the kitchen counter, Maria.

MARIA *and* STAMATIS *head towards the house.*

HARVEY. And, Maria…

MARIA. Yes, Mr?

HARVEY. Tell your father that tomorrow morning at eleven we'll meet him in town, by his brother's tobacco shop.

MARIA. I will say to him.

HARVEY. And then Mr Manning and myself will take him to a lawyer's so that we can get the whole thing sorted quickly and efficiently.

THEO. You don't need to come.

HARVEY. Greek lawyers, Theo, Greek bureaucracy, trust me, you need me there. And I know the lingo.

MARIA *smiles at* HARVEY.

MARIA. Thank you, Mr.

HARVEY. You're very welcome.

*She turns to* STAMATIS.

MARIA. *Έλα πατέρα, πάμε για το Ουίσκι!* [Come, Dad, let's get the whisky.]

*And they run into the house.*

*For a second, nobody says a word. Then* JUNE *shrieks.*

JUNE. Oh my God, you own this house! You own this house! You own this house!

THEO *too is suddenly overwhelmed.*

THEO. We do, it's true, we do. Charlotte, we own this house!

*He kisses her. She attempts to partake, for him, but it's difficult.*

CHARLOTTE. I know we do, I know we do.

THEO. It's good, Charlotte, it's good. Whatever you're feeling now, I know it's good!

CHARLOTTE. Maybe, yes, probably.

HARVEY. It is, Charlotte, for God's sake, lighten up and live this glorious moment!

JUNE. Oh, Charlotte, it's wonderful! So wonderful!

CHARLOTTE. Yes.

JUNE. Can I kiss you, can I kiss you both?

THEO. I've been waiting all evening, June.

*She kisses them.*

JUNE. Just think, all the summers you'll have here.

HARVEY. To rest, and play, and *work*, Theo.

THEO. To work, yes!

*HARVEY hugs him. He goes up to* CHARLOTTE, *opens his arms.*

HARVEY. May I?

*She doesn't reply, just looks at him.*

Jesus, woman, put down your defences for just one moment.

*She lets him, he hugs her. At first she resists and it's awkward but then she gives in and the moment is sexually charged. JUNE notices; THEO is oblivious. Then HARVEY ends the embrace. When he speaks, it is with some feeling.*

Blessed be this house and all that live in it.

*Then MARIA comes running out of the house, in a state of some excitement.*

MARIA. Mr Manning, Mrs Manning!

CHARLOTTE. What is it, Maria? Is everything all right?

MARIA. It's the radio!

CHARLOTTE. What about the radio?

MARIA. It's the… how you call it, the *nea*.

HARVEY. The news.

MARIA. There has been in Athens this morning a big thing. With tanks.

THEO. Tanks? What kind of tanks?

MARIA. With the Government. They have thrown them out with tanks. There has been, I don't know how you say in English…

HARVEY. It's a French word, Maria, well, technically three.

MARIA. Come, come and listen. Please, come.

JUNE. Okay, sweetheart, we'll come and listen to the news.

THEO. Jesus. A bloody coup is what she means!

*THEO and JUNE follow an excited MARIA into the house, JUNE throwing a slightly worried look over her shoulder at leaving HARVEY alone with CHARLOTTE. CHARLOTTE begins to make her way towards the house too, as the penny starts to drop. HARVEY hovers, knowing what's coming.*

*Eventually, she stops, and turns to him.*

CHARLOTTE. I thought you were a fan of democracy.

HARVEY. I am, Charlotte, more than you'll ever know.

*Pause.*

But democracy is a work in progress.

CHARLOTTE *lets out a little laugh.*

I don't like the means any more than you do but they *will* be justified one day, mark my words.

CHARLOTTE. Keep saying that to yourself, otherwise how do you look in the mirror every morning?

HARVEY. With great difficulty, Charlotte, so please don't be glib.

*Pause.*

Have you ever heard a man screaming under extreme and devastating physical pain?

CHARLOTTE. I can't say I have.

HARVEY. I'm happy for you, I hope you never have to.

*Pause.*

It's high-pitched and insistent, something like an animal in the middle of the dark night.

*Pause.*

I have heard those screams walking down subterranean corridors in strange small countries that you would have some difficulty finding on a map. I have heard them and taken them with me, ringing in my ears and my soul, so that you will never have to.

CHARLOTTE. Why?

HARVEY. Because, Charlotte, whether you are aware of it or not, we are at war for the soul of the world, and I, for one, care about the outcome.

CHARLOTTE. That fills me with hope. The outcome you plan to bring about.

*HARVEY talks slowly and with a quiet, dangerous steel in his voice.*

HARVEY. I am up to my elbows in dirt, and blood, and grime, Charlotte, so that you and Theo and people like you can carry on living the way you are. So that Theo can write his plays and you can act in them and then the two of you can stand on this terrace at the end of a day of clean work and bask in the feeling that you are good people. So please, as a token of your appreciation, try at least to give me a little due respect.

CHARLOTTE. And how can I do that?

HARVEY. Begin by using your imagination and refusing to think in a lazy and convenient way. It's lazy and convenient for you to consider me some sort of sociopath just as it's lazy and convenient for you to believe that all the fine things you have in your life do not come with a very hefty price. But I am the one, Charlotte, who will defend you and the way you live. And I ask you only one favour.

CHARLOTTE. Which is?

HARVEY. That you remember this. I too am a good man. A good man who has done – and does – certain things for which he feels a terrible remorse. Things which will revisit me over and over again in both my waking and my sleeping hours, and will continue to do so until my dying breath.

CHARLOTTE. So why do you do these things?

HARVEY. Because I believe in something.

*When CHARLOTTE speaks, it is with sarcasm.*

CHARLOTTE. What do you believe in, Harvey? Democracy?

HARVEY. I believe in never capitulating my will, my reason, or my imagination, to any authority – neither so-called sacred or temporal – which expects me to stop thinking, questioning, *demanding* answers. It's who I am, Charlotte.

*Pause.*

What do you believe in, Charlotte? Unicorns?

*He walks up to her. For a few seconds they just stand there, dangerously close to each other, neither of them moves.*

Why did I turn around to you at that café on the port and start the conversation yesterday morning?

CHARLOTTE. I don't know, why did you?

HARVEY. Because, Charlotte, I was attracted to you. Quite overwhelmingly, the force of it took me by surprise.

*Pause.*

And why did you then ask me and my wife over for drinks at your house?

CHARLOTTE. Why?

HARVEY. Because you felt exactly the same way.

*Pause.*

I'm a man, you're a woman, nature, that sort of thing, it happens. But you've decided to live with a child, and who can blame you? Who wouldn't want to live with a child when you know the things that men are capable of? Do you know, if I was that way inclined, I too would rather fancy the idea of spending my life with Theo Manning.

*Pause.*

So we are attracted to each other and nothing will ever come of it because we will not permit it. You love Theo and I think I'm beginning to love him as well and we do not want to hurt him. He is too precious. And I don't want to hurt June either, because she has been loyal to me through thick and thin and has comforted me when I have woken her with my own screams in the middle of the night, soaked in a pool of sweat. So nothing will ever come of it – that's where the will part comes in handy.

*Pause.*

You are a good woman, Charlotte, and I am a good man.

*Pause.*

So now it has been named, we can put it away for ever and all of us can be friends.

THEO *comes running out,* HARVEY *and* CHARLOTTE *automatically move apart.*

THEO. It's true, it's on the World Service, there's been some sort of a right-wing coup, some colonels or something have taken over. Charlotte, come, Harvey, come and listen!

CHARLOTTE *makes her way towards the house, shaken.* HARVEY *stands where he is, he does not move.*

Harvey, don't you want to listen to the news?

CHARLOTTE. I think Harvey may know the news already, darling.

*And she enters the house.*

HARVEY *still doesn't move, he is lost in thought.* THEO *starts to make his way towards him.*

THEO. Harvey, there's been some sort of a coup, the military has taken over.

HARVEY. Was there bloodletting, violence? Were many killed?

THEO. Doesn't sound like it, not much resistance at all, they just marched in, unchallenged.

HARVEY. Good. I mean good that there wasn't much blood.

THEO. Still, Christ. A coup.

HARVEY. Yes.

*Pause.*

THEO. Puts a bit of a damper on buying this house.

HARVEY. Does it?

THEO. Well, what I mean is, who wants to own a house in a military dictatorship?

HARVEY. The island won't be affected. Nothing will change here. Life will go on as usual.

THEO. I know, but still, as *a feeling*. It doesn't feel right.

*HARVEY smiles to himself.*

HARVEY. Ah, yes, as *a feeling*.

*Pause.*

Anyway, don't worry, it won't last for ever. It's transitional.
A few years maybe. Just until things settle down. And
compared to your South Americans, they're a little
lightweight this lot, bordering on the ridiculous. I wouldn't
worry too much about it.

THEO. How do you know these things?

HARVEY. Just guessing.

*Pause.*

So what are you going to call the house?

THEO. Call it?

HARVEY. This house needs a name.

THEO. It does?

HARVEY. Every house needs a name, Theo.

THEO. If you say so.

*Pause.*

HARVEY. I know.

THEO. What?

HARVEY. Your Muse, name it after your Muse.

THEO. My Muse?

HARVEY. Yes, Theo. Make her feel wanted, welcome,
cherished and appreciated.

THEO. I like that.

HARVEY. Put a chair in the corner, there for her, and name the
house after her so she will always feel at home by your side.

THEO. Okay, the Muse, yes. So I just call the house 'Muse', do I? That sounds a little strange.

HARVEY. No, you call the house Villa Thalia.

THEO. That's even stranger.

HARVEY. Why is it stranger?

THEO. Well, for a start, it's not really a villa, it's more of a peasant shack.

HARVEY. You're a writer, Charlotte's an actress and once you stock up the bar and offer people dry Martinis and whisky sours, it will be a villa.

THEO. And then, of course, Thalia…

HARVEY. Is the Muse of Comedy, yes.

THEO. But I don't really write comedies, or aspire to.

HARVEY. But you should, Theo. A fine comedy is an exquisite thing. I don't mean a farce, adulterous English folk running around with their pants around their ankles…

THEO. No, that's not really my style.

HARVEY. But something satirical, Theo, and provocative, and funny.

*Pause.* THEO *considers it for a minute. Then looks at the house over his shoulder, almost as if to check that* CHARLOTTE *isn't listening.*

THEO. Okay then, Villa Thalia. For you. In honour of the man who made it happen.

HARVEY *smiles, with bittersweet irony.*

HARVEY. Thank you.

THEO. Come, we need to listen to the news, we need to know what's happening.

*And he makes his way towards the house.*

HARVEY. In a moment.

THEO *goes back into the house.*

*But* HARVEY *remains where he is, staring out at the sunset, and the sea.*

*Lights fade to darkness.*

*End of Act One.*

## ACT TWO

*The scene is now nine years later and there have been some
alterations to the terrace – an awning, a painted door, an outside
light, a splashing of tiles. And the furniture that is scattered
across the space – a couple of tables, some sunloungers, are all
new too. Even though underneath the more Europeanised feel of
the place one can still discern the rustic quality that the house
once had, it can now be categorised quite easily as a 1970s
holiday villa, albeit of a slightly bohemian quality.*

*And there is nothing luxurious or ordered about this villa – at
this moment in time, it appears very lived in, almost messy.
The terrace is scattered with the usual summer-holiday
paraphernalia – beach towels, random flip-flops, two rackets
and a ball, a beach umbrella leaning precariously against
a wall. There is a clothes horse in a corner with lots of summer
clothes drying on it. And somewhere on the edge, there is also
a cassette recorder too, and a box of cassettes by it.*

*And on a small table somewhere,* THEO*'s Corona, and next to
it, pages under a large stone.*

*It is a late afternoon in August, 1976.*

ADRIAN *and* ROSALIND *are stretched out on the ground in
swimsuits and T-shirts, reading children's books.*

JUNE *walks on. Her clothes and hair are of a very different
style to when we last saw her – very seventies now, and casual,
summery. But whatever it is she is wearing, her shoulders are
bare. She is holding a small bottle of nail varnish in one hand
and a glass of Bacardi in the other.*

JUNE. Hello, sweetnesses.

   *The children look up.*

ADRIAN. Hello, Mrs Parker.

JUNE. Honey, how many times have I told you to call me June, I'm not a schoolteacher, I'm your friend.

ADRIAN. Hello, June.

JUNE. That's better. Look at you both reading your books, aren't you just the most adorable things! What's that, what are you reading, honey?

*ADRIAN shows her the cover of the book.*

ADRIAN. *Five Have a Mystery to Solve*, I told you earlier.

JUNE. Oh, that's right, you did, but you know, sweetheart, you have to be told things more than once when you're my age and you like Bacardi.

*She positions one of the sunloungers so that it faces the sun, aims for the right angle, moves it around a bit.*

Just ignore me, I'm going to do my nails, God knows they need it.

ADRIAN. All right, we'll ignore you.

*JUNE sits down, unscrews the bottle of nail varnish, rests one of her feet on the edge of the sunlounger and begins working on her toenails.*

*CHARLOTTE strolls on, holding an empty basket. She is there to take the dry clothes off the clothes horse – for the next few minutes and as she chats, she takes the items off one by one, folds them on the table, and places them all into the basket.*

*THEO follows her on, but he carries a tray with a large jug of something red and some floating fruit in it, and a few glasses. He rests the tray on the table.*

CHARLOTTE. Children, time to get out of your swimsuits and get dressed for supper.

ADRIAN. But Harvey promised he'd take us for a swim, Mummy!

JUNE. Well, maybe you should go remind him, sweetheart, he needs a nudge.

ROSALIND. Can we go, Mummy?

CHARLOTTE. Maybe Harvey's changed his mind, darling.

JUNE. A promise is a promise, go get him, kids.

CHARLOTTE. Are you sure?

JUNE. I'm positive, he needs to be dragged out of that room, he's being morose.

CHARLOTTE. All right then, but it will be a quick one, five minutes, it's gone six o'clock.

ADRIAN. Yes, Mummy!

*The children start to run off in a state of some excitement, ROSALIND grabs a pair of armbands as she goes and hands them to THEO.*

ROSALIND. Blow them up for me, Daddy!

THEO. Please, yes I may.

ROSALIND. Please! Thank you!

*And the children run off. THEO starts to blow up the armbands. CHARLOTTE continues to fold the clean clothes. JUNE is concentrating avidly on her toenails.*

THEO. I've made some of that fruit punch you like so much, June.

JUNE. Oh, Theo, I love that stuff, thank you, all punch and no fruit.

CHARLOTTE. I don't know why you call it fruit punch. More of a sangria really, half a gallon of red wine in there.

THEO. And a pint of rum.

JUNE. Yummy.

CHARLOTTE. Did you manage a siesta?

JUNE. Not really, I had to finish the packing, then Harvey seems tense, pacing up and down like a predatory animal, he was making me nervous, you try snoozing with that in the room.

THEO. Why is he tense?

JUNE. Why is it hot in Greece, Theo? Why do those cicada things never shut up?

CHARLOTTE. I noticed he hardly said a word at lunch.

JUNE. I think something happened last night.

THEO. Happened, what happened?

JUNE. I wish I knew, Theo. When we went into the port to get the newspapers and some cigarettes, he left me in a bar for half an hour, then when he came back again he was being weird, sullen, and just plain moody.

CHARLOTTE. How strange.

JUNE. Maybe something he read in the papers, God knows, or some depressing thought he had. And then that phone call this morning didn't help.

THEO. Bad news?

JUNE. They want him in Kinshasa next week, can you imagine? His heart sank when he heard. The Congo, for God's sake, or Zaire or whatever its name is these days. He hates that place.

CHARLOTTE. Duty calls.

THEO. But you've had a good holiday? Restful, at least.

JUNE. Oh, God, we've loved it, Theo, even if it was just a few days. Just being here with you and Charlotte, and those gorgeous children of yours, I could eat them!

CHARLOTTE. I'd rather you didn't.

JUNE *stops with the nails for a second, touches her right shoulder with her left hand.*

JUNE. My shoulders are burnt, I should have listened to you, Charlotte.

*And then she's back at the toenails again.*

THEO *has finished with the armbands, he puts them down, and stands.*

THEO. Right, before I start indulging, I'm going to do my exercises. Just ignore me, ladies.

*He starts doing some squats.*

CHARLOTTE. Why do you insist on doing those in public every evening?

THEO. Because I need to exhibit my virile manhood.

JUNE. I can't see it, Theo. I keep looking for it when you're doing those squats but I can never see it.

CHARLOTTE. When he does them in his briefs, it pops out from time to time.

JUNE. How wonderful.

CHARLOTTE. But you need to get quite close. It's like a cheeky little goldfish.

THEO. Don't listen to her, June, it's a barracuda.

ADRIAN *and* ROSALIND *drag* HARVEY *on. He's in shorts and a T-shirt, looking more haggard than when we last saw him. He too has had a couple of drinks and there's a bit of an edge to him. He comes on with a slightly forced joviality.*

ROSALIND. We found him!

HARVEY. They found me!

JUNE. There you are.

ADRIAN. He was hiding!

HARVEY. But your agents are effective.

JUNE. Have you packed your bags yet, Harvey?

HARVEY. Yes, dear. So this is where the party is. Nice to see you working on those quadriceps, Theo, they need a little firming, I noticed that earlier.

THEO. I am a man of steel.

HARVEY. I've been coerced into joining you. Well, physically forced.

JUNE. Stops you brooding, mister.

HARVEY. I expect it's a good thing. I grew sick of arguing with myself, I need external stimuli if only for amusement.

CHARLOTTE. We'll do our best.

THEO *has finished his squats and now throws himself into push-ups*.

THEO. What were you arguing about?

HARVEY. This place seems to have that effect on me, it makes me introspective.

CHARLOTTE. That can't be a bad thing.

JUNE. Well, at least you're a little livelier now than you were last night and this morning.

HARVEY. I'm doing my best, June.

JUNE (*watching* THEO *doing his push-ups*). You look very sexy when you're doing those, Theo.

THEO. Thank you, June, I believe I do.

HARVEY *pours himself a glass of the punch and raises his glass*.

HARVEY. And so the time is fast approaching when we shall say goodbye, it breaks my heart.

THEO. We've liked having you, Harvey.

HARVEY. Thank you, Theo, that's kind of you to say.

THEO. I mean it.

JUNE. Harvey, the kids are waiting for that swim you promised them.

THEO'*s push-ups are over. He jumps up*.

THEO. Right, and a few sit-ups and we're done.

*He's down again, doing the sit-ups*.

HARVEY. I know you mean it, Theo, I'd never doubt it. At least we offer novelty value, if nothing else. I mean from what you have pointed out a few times over the last few days, Charlotte, most of your friends are artists like yourselves, well, actors, writers, directors, *theatre folk*, June, theatricals if you like, that sort of thing.

JUNE. Well, that makes sense, it's their world.

HARVEY. So to have us two under your roof must be an exception, we're different animals altogether, aren't we, June?

JUNE. Speak for yourself, I'm a human being, not a hyena. Did you see that after-sun cream in the room, Harvey? I need some for my shoulders.

HARVEY *claps his hands.*

HARVEY. Right, is it time to head to the beach, kiddos?

ROSALIND/ADRIAN. Yes! Yes, it is!

HARVEY *and the children start to make their way towards the path that leads to the beach. But on his way, HARVEY passes by the pages of THEO's new play sitting next to the typewriter. He places his hand on it.*

HARVEY. A good day's work, Theo?

THEO *has finished his sit-ups, the exercises are over. He walks over to the punch, and pours himself a glass.*

THEO. Not bad. Done some rewrites on the second scene and started on Act Two.

HARVEY. I'm happy to hear it.

CHARLOTTE. He was up at five with the cockerels.

THEO. I got a couple of hours in. And then a little more when you all went off to the taverna for lunch.

HARVEY. Good man.

JUNE. You're so industrious, Theo, it's admirable.

HARVEY. He has a vocation, June, a calling.

THEO. I don't know if it's that.

JUNE. I have a vocation too.

CHARLOTTE. For what, June?

JUNE. For breathing. I have a calling towards inhaling oxygen, I can't help it, I do.

HARVEY. But seriously, can I just have a moment here?

*Suddenly inspired,* HARVEY *pulls out a chair and jumps onto it.*

JUNE. Why are you standing on the chair, sweetheart?

HARVEY. In order to create an atmosphere of awe and ceremony. I need you to listen to me now with some attention and just a little reverence. This is serious, folks.

ADRIAN. Harvey, come on, let's go swimming!

HARVEY. One minute, kids, one minute, that's all, I promise you.

*He takes a moment to find the right words and when he does he speaks with sincerity and some emotion.*

Isn't it extraordinary how things worked out for you? Was I right or was I right about you, Theo?

THEO. Right about what?

HARVEY. This place, Theo, this house.

THEO. What about it, Harvey?

HARVEY. Nine years ago, Theo, in 1967, when we were younger and just a little less tired, we all stood where we are now, and do you remember what I said to you?

JUNE. You said many things, sweetheart, you always do.

HARVEY. But do you remember what I said more than anything else?

THEO. What did you say, Harvey?

HARVEY (*with some passion*). I said that you were going to be a successful and important writer. I said that somehow, buying this house, making it your own, writing here – *here*, Theo, here, at this exact spot – was going to help you become the writer you were always destined to be.

THEO. You did.

HARVEY. Thank you. And then it happened.

THEO. Did it?

HARVEY. And I am proud of that. I mean, of the very small part I played in that process, in making that come to be.

CHARLOTTE. Harvey, could you get off that chair, please? They're quite delicate, those chairs, fragile.

HARVEY. You even wrote a comedy, Theo. You said you never would but you did.

THEO. It was a critical catastrophe, thank you for the suggestion. *The Times* said, and I quote, that 'the play came into its own at the curtain call'.

HARVEY. But the public queued around the block and sometimes the public know a thing or two.

THEO. It was the coldest winter on record, the Criterion is famously warm.

HARVEY. And you have grown, as a writer, Theo and expanded, and your voice has become stronger and more confident, and it *has* changed things, damn it.

THEO. 'Changed things'? What things?

CHARLOTTE. Please get off the chair, Harvey.

HARVEY. Your plays are quietly political, Theo, and even though their politics may lean a little too much to the left for my liking, well, damn it, you have a way of coaxing people towards broadening their sympathies and that, my friend, can only be a good thing in this screwed-up world of ours.

THEO. Thank you, Harvey, enough now.

JUNE. He's right, Theo, your plays are always moving.

CHARLOTTE (*still about the chair*). Harvey, please.

HARVEY. Well, it's interesting you use that word, June, because you know I was thinking the other day that to *move* someone, well, yes it means, you make them feel something, you inspire some sort of emotional response in them, you elicit sympathy, I don't know, *empathy*, but it also means that you *reposition* them, they have a new perspective, a new angle, they have been *moved*.

JUNE. God, you're right, Harvey, I'd never thought of it like that.

HARVEY. And you have done that, Theo. Writing here. In *this* place. You have repositioned us.

*Pause*.

So I was right. That's all.

THEO. If you say so.

HARVEY *jumps off the chair*.

HARVEY. And that chair is doing just fine, Charlotte.

*Turns to the children*.

Come on, kids, let's have that swim.

JUNE. That was beautiful, honey, if a little strange.

CHARLOTTE *has finished folding the clothes*.

CHARLOTTE. It's true what you say about Theo's work.

THEO. Thank you, darling.

CHARLOTTE. But you exaggerate the role this house has played.

*She picks up the basket of folded clothes and starts to move towards the house*.

Don't get me wrong, we have loved it here…

HARVEY. *Have* loved it?

CHARLOTTE. But if it hadn't been this place, it would have been somewhere else.

HARVEY. I don't think so, Charlotte.

CHARLOTTE. Well, I do.

*And she enters the house with the basket.* HARVEY *is riled but does his best to conceal it.* ROSALIND *is now pulling him by the hand,* ADRIAN *joins her at it.*

ROSALIND/ADRIAN. Harvey! Come on, Harvey!

JUNE. Well, either way, it's a wonderful holiday home and that's all that matters.

HARVEY. It's more than that. Did you not listen to what I said, June?

ROSALIND. Come on, Harvey!

ADRIAN. Harvey, it's going to be too late to swim!

JUNE. If you're going to take the kids swimming, Harvey, you better do it now.

ROSALIND. Harvey, you promised!

HARVEY. Okay then, come on, kids, let's go and have that final swim.

THEO. A quick one, kids, five minutes, that's all!

*They start to go.*

Armbands!

ROSALIND *goes and grabs them, then follows* HARVEY *and* ADRIAN *as they head towards the beach. But* HARVEY *stops for a second, looks at* THEO.

HARVEY. You understand me, though, Theo, don't you?

THEO. I'm trying, Harvey.

JUNE. Sweetheart, before you disappear, can you fetch me that bottle of after-sun cream from the room?

*But they've gone.*

I think that's a no.

*She stands.*

I need some of that stuff on my shoulders.

*She starts to wander off to get the cream.*

You see, what I mean, he's being so weird, I don't know what it is.

*And she goes.*

THEO *is left alone.*

*He walks over to the table and picks up a Polaroid camera that is resting on it, next to a sheet of paper and a tape measure. He starts moving around the terrace, taking photographs of it, and of the house, from every angle.*

CHARLOTTE *returns. She goes to the clothes horse and starts to fold it away.*

CHARLOTTE. Where is everyone?

THEO. Harvey's taken the kids for that swim. And June's getting something from her room.

CHARLOTTE *approaches* THEO, *speaks quietly and with urgency, looking over her shoulder to make sure she isn't being heard.*

CHARLOTTE. I can't do this again.

THEO *keeps taking photographs.*

THEO. You invited them.

CHARLOTTE. They didn't give me a choice. She said, 'We're in Athens for a few weeks, we'll take the ferry and come see you.' They invited themselves, Theo, you know that.

THEO. I believe you.

CHARLOTTE. Why are we their friends? What have we got in common?

THEO. Not a lot. But is that a bad thing?

CHARLOTTE. Never again.

*She looks at him taking the photographs.*

Why are you taking photos?

THEO. For the Bauers. Gustav said they'd like some to show their architects in Hamburg. A few changes they want to make. And I measured everything this morning, it's on that sheet of paper over there.

*He points over to the piece of paper.*

CHARLOTTE. Don't do that now, do it tomorrow.

THEO. I want to post it off in the morning. Gustav said the architect needs them by next week. I can stop at the post office on the way back from the port.

CHARLOTTE. It can wait, Theo. I don't want them to know.

THEO. Know what?

CHARLOTTE. About the house, about the Bauers. I don't want them to know.

THEO. It's fine, I'm not going to tell them, we said we wouldn't.

CHARLOTTE. You saw what he's like about it. Sentimental.

THEO. Some of what he said was true, I think.

CHARLOTTE. Just put them away somewhere. And the measurements.

THEO *places the photos and measurements under a flower pot so that they won't blow away.*

JUNE *comes back, after-sun cream in hand.*

JUNE. I'm sore all over but at least I'm grilled and ready for the fall.

THEO. What fall?

JUNE. I mean the autumn, Theo, not my personal decline.

THEO *stands in front of her with the camera.*

THEO. Smile!

JUNE. Wait! Give a woman a chance.

*She touches up her hair a bit, poses.*

Ready!

*He takes the photo.*

THEO. Something to remember you by.

JUNE. You make it sound like I'm about to die. Oh, wait, and I want one with my friend Charlotte.

*She beckons* CHARLOTTE.

Come on, Charlotte, stand here, next to me!

CHARLOTTE *joins her reluctantly.* JUNE *puts her arm around* CHARLOTTE's *shoulder, there is a slight awkwardness to the moment.*

Me and my friend Charlotte.

CHARLOTTE. Go on, Theo. Take the photograph.

THEO *takes it.* CHARLOTTE *moves quickly, releasing herself from the pose.*

I should go take that stew thing off the hob.

THEO. I'll do it.

CHARLOTTE *is annoyed – she wanted an escape. But* THEO, *who also doesn't want to be left alone with* JUNE, *has already put the camera and the photos down on the table and is moving towards the house.* CHARLOTTE *gives him an accusing look as he goes.*

JUNE *pours herself a glass of punch, then moves back towards sunlounger, perches on it, takes the lid off the after-sun cream.*

JUNE. Can you do my shoulders for me, Charlotte?

CHARLOTTE. Of course.

*But she's not that effective at hiding the fact she'd rather not.*

CHARLOTTE *walks over to where* JUNE *is and takes the bottle from her. She pours some cream into her hand and starts to apply it onto* JUNE's *shoulders.*

JUNE. That bit is sore, serves me right.

*For a few seconds, they continue like this,* CHARLOTTE *rubbing cream into* JUNE, JUNE *sipping her punch.*

We haven't really had any girl time, have we?

CHARLOTTE. I suppose not.

JUNE. What with those men around, and the kids. I mean, don't get me wrong, I love their company, but the two of us haven't had a chance, have we?

CHARLOTTE *doesn't say anything, just keeps applying the cream.*

I know we could have gone for a walk or something, but I felt that maybe you didn't want to...

CHARLOTTE. It isn't that, it's just, well, you know...

JUNE. Of course, I understand.

*For a few seconds they continue in silence,* CHARLOTTE *applying the cream onto* JUNE*'s back.*

I'm frightened of him. And frightened *for* him. I don't know which. Both.

*She waits for something from* CHARLOTTE *but doesn't get it. So she perseveres.*

You don't know the half of it, Charlotte. You don't know how bad it is.

*And suddenly* JUNE *stands up, and steps away from her, overcome by a sudden burst of emotion.*

Oh, God.

*She puts her hand to her mouth, lets out a little sob. Then turns back to* CHARLOTTE, *pulls herself together.*

I'm sorry.

CHARLOTTE *is disconcerted, doesn't how to respond.* JUNE *begins to talk with some urgency, knowing she hasn't much time.*

Certain things… I couldn't even tell my mother, Charlotte, *especially* my mother, and my friends, the girls back home, they wouldn't understand, oh God, I'm scared.

CHARLOTTE (*tentatively, knowing she's opening a can of worms*). What are you scared of?

JUNE. But you're different, you and Theo are *different*, you'd understand.

*Again,* JUNE *checks to see nobody is listening, as if about to impart a terrible secret. She comes back to the sunlounger, sits next to* CHARLOTTE.

You know we're not together, any more.

CHARLOTTE. Not together?

JUNE. Not *sexually*, I mean, Charlotte, he hasn't fucked me in six months and before that it was like… well, it wasn't fun, not like he wanted to is what I mean, it's been like that for a very long time.

CHARLOTTE. I see.

JUNE. I mean even after we found out we couldn't… we weren't going to have children, well, even then for some time, there was some enjoyment, we were still, you know…

CHARLOTTE. June, I really –

JUNE. But then it all stopped, after Chile.

CHARLOTTE. Chile?

JUNE. After our time in Santiago. That's when it happened, Charlotte, that's when he changed.

THEO *comes out.*

THEO. It needs a bit longer, but I've put it on a low heat.

*There is an awkward moment.*

CHARLOTTE. Theo, could you slice those tomatoes. The ones on the counter. For the salad, I mean. And then put them in the fridge.

THEO. Now? Surely we can do that later.

CHARLOTTE. No, *now*, Theo.

*And he gets it.*

THEO. Oh, yes. Of course.

*He goes back into the house.* JUNE *stands, moves to the table, grabs her Virginia Slims, lights one.*

JUNE. The situation was very bad, I'm sure you read about it, everything fell apart, the whole place was in chaos and then there was the coup, and then all the other stuff.

CHARLOTTE. Other stuff?

JUNE. But we were there for the whole thing, I mean Harvey was living through it every day –

CHARLOTTE. He was a part of it.

JUNE. So they put us up in this apartment in this fancy area of Santiago, and it was perfectly nice, I mean it was a middle-class neighbourhood, there were parks nearby, a couple of cafés, and the apartment itself was elegant, tall ceilings, beautiful parquet floors, that sort of thing.

CHARLOTTE. How lovely.

JUNE. And there was this woman who lived next door with her son. So we got to know her, well, both of them really, they even came over for dinner one night. She was a music teacher, she taught music at a local girls' school and he was… the son, well he was in his twenties and he was a pianist, Charlotte, he was training to be a concert pianist. He was a beautiful boy, black curly hair, and strong too, but his hands were the hands of a pianist.

CHARLOTTE. All right.

JUNE. Sometimes we'd hear him practise through the walls, Bach, Mozart, Chopin, you name it, and he played so beautifully and the walls were thin, so you could hear it, but it never disturbed us, because he was *good*, and you know

Harvey would actually put his chair near the wall so that he could hear it even better. So it never bothered us is what I mean, because he played so well.

CHARLOTTE. Why are you telling me all this?

JUNE. Well, then he went missing. The boy went missing, Charlotte.

*Pause.*

It was madness, you have to understand. Because even if you read about it in the papers you will never comprehend what was going on there. It was pandemonium, and things had to be done to save the country, it was that bad.

CHARLOTTE. Things were bad after the coup you mean?

JUNE. No, I mean *before* the coup, Charlotte, the country was in free fall, economically, socially, every which way, that man Allende was a Marxist and he was taking the country to hell in a hand basket. But anyway, in the few days after the coup, things happened, people were gathered up, you know, *communists*, I mean, people who were trying to destroy… well, people who were dangerous, Charlotte, a lot of them were anarchists and worse, but there's no denying that in that effort to quash… in that effort to return the country to safety, mistakes were made, because there was chaos, and the Chileans themselves, well, they can be disorganised, impulsive, like children, it's in their blood. So terrible things happened, there's no denying.

CHARLOTTE. What happened to the boy?

JUNE. There was a football stadium, Charlotte, the army gathered people in it, and then afterwards, many went missing. And he was one of them.

CHARLOTTE. And then what?

JUNE. Well, the mother, she went crazy, wouldn't you have done? She'd shuffle around in her slippers all day and all night calling his name, like she was looking for him, expecting him to pop out, I don't know, from behind the

wardrobe or something, and we could hear it, she'd be
calling his name all day and all night, '*Gabriel, Gabriel,
dónde estás?*'

CHARLOTTE. Where are you?

JUNE. Harvey started playing records so that we wouldn't have
to listen to her. Jazz, for Christ's sake, and Burt Bacharach
and God knows what else, so that we wouldn't have to listen
to this woman calling her son's name.

*Pause.*

And the thing is, Charlotte, he wasn't even a communist.
He was young, that's all, idealistic, I suppose, a *kind* boy,
sensitive. He got caught up in it all, I expect, took a few bad
turns, was in the wrong place at the wrong time.

*And* JUNE *realises she's gone too far, decides to pull back
a little.*

But at least the country was saved, that's the one good thing.

CHARLOTTE. Was it?

JUNE. So that's when it all started falling apart. And that's
when the paranoia started.

CHARLOTTE. What paranoia, June?

JUNE. He just started getting these weird ideas, like he was
being followed all the time, every time he got in the car his
eyes would be glued to the rear-view mirror and then he'd
get jumpy in restaurants or walking down the street, like he
was expecting someone to leap out from behind a bush or
something and put a bullet to his head. And the last few
weeks it's been unbearable, of course.

CHARLOTTE. Why's that?

JUNE. Well, remember he said he got called back to Athens
because they assassinated that guy from the Embassy in
December?

CHARLOTTE. He's investigating it, yes.

JUNE. Well, the more he's been working on all that, the more nervous he's become, like an animal being hunted. He even asked the security guys at the Embassy for a gun, it's horrible.

CHARLOTTE. A gun?

JUNE. He carries it with him everywhere now. But it's crazy, I mean, we're coming here, and I'm like, 'We're going to stay with friends on an island, Harvey, you don't need that thing with you, it's crazy.'

*CHARLOTTE is in shock; she stands.*

CHARLOTTE. He has a gun here? In this house?

JUNE. Don't worry, it doesn't mean anything, it's like a state of mind.

CHARLOTTE. 'A state of mind'?

*She moves towards the house, begins to shout THEO's name.*

Theo, Theo!

JUNE. Charlotte, please!

CHARLOTTE. I don't want a gun in this house!

JUNE. For God's sake, Charlotte, we're leaving in the morning.

CHARLOTTE. Theo!

JUNE. It doesn't mean a thing.

CHARLOTTE. So why does he have it then, and why did you tell me?

*THEO emerges from the house. He's wearing an apron, holds a tomato in one hand, a sharp knife in the other.*

THEO. What's wrong?

JUNE. Charlotte, please, I told you in confidence!

CHARLOTTE. I'm sorry, June, but I don't like it, I don't like it one bit.

THEO. Don't like what, what's happening?

JUNE. Charlotte, please.

CHARLOTTE. Not in this house, not with children here, you should have told us.

THEO. Told us what?

CHARLOTTE. I just don't like it!

*JUNE points at THEO who is standing there with a knife in his hand.*

JUNE. I mean, look at Theo, he's holding a knife, he's not going to use it to kill someone.

CHARLOTTE. That's not the same, June.

JUNE. Why isn't it the same?

CHARLOTTE. Because he's slicing tomatoes with it.

THEO. Who's going to kill someone?

JUNE. No, but what I mean is, he's not going to use it any more than Theo is going to use that knife.

THEO. I am using the knife.

JUNE. Not to kill someone is what I mean.

THEO. Kill who?

CHARLOTTE. Oh, for God's sake! This is my house and there are children here. I'm sorry, June, for what's happened, and I'm sorry that Harvey is paranoid or whatever you want to call it, but I do not want a gun in this house.

THEO. Harvey's got a gun?

*And HARVEY suddenly runs on with ADRIAN and ROSALIND in tow. He jumps up behind THEO, THEO turns and HARVEY sees the knife in THEO's hand. He screams, hamming it up.*

HARVEY. No! No, please don't kill me! I'm sorry I insulted your quadriceps! Please don't kill me with that tomato!

JUNE. Harvey!

*Pause. JUNE looks at CHARLOTTE, pleadingly.*

Charlotte, I beg you.

HARVEY. Beg her what?

JUNE. We're leaving in the morning, we'll be out of your hair for good.

HARVEY. Are you sick of having us?

*Pause.* CHARLOTTE *decides to keep quiet.*

CHARLOTTE. Right, Theo, you better get back to those tomatoes and let's forget it all.

THEO. Do I have to?

HARVEY. Oh, that's what the knife is for, what a relief!

CHARLOTTE *goes to the table, pours herself a glass of punch.* THEO *hovers.*

JUNE. That was a quick swim.

HARVEY. Well, we got excited about something else, didn't we, kids?

ADRIAN. Harvey's going to teach us how to Greek dance!

JUNE. Oh, for God's sake, Harvey.

HARVEY. I think it's appropriate, on our last day here, to do something in celebration of the spirit of this beautiful country. Where's that tape you were listening to the other night, Theo? You know, the Greek one.

THEO. Should be there, by the cassette recorder.

HARVEY *makes his way over to where the recorder is, starts to shuffle through all the different cassettes.*

HARVEY. Because that's another thing we've not discussed, let alone celebrated.

THEO. What's that?

HARVEY (*still rummaging through the tapes*). When we first met on this island, all those many years ago, it happened to be on the unfortunate day that the colonels came to power, remember, Charlotte? And here we are, ten years later, and those very same colonels are rotting in jail somewhere, they served their purpose, the communist threat was averted, and we are now holidaying in what this country was always destined to be – a shining beacon of modern democracy. Isn't that a wonderful thing?

*He has found the tape he's looking for.*

Ah, here it is, I believe this is the one.

*He takes whatever tape is in the recorder out, and replaces it with the Greek one. He presses play. The music begins and it is a* rebetiko *song, 'Fragosiriani', plaintive and beautiful.*

So, kids, in honour of the resilient spirit of this nation and its people and their return to civilisation, I am going to teach you the rudiments of Greek dancing.

JUNE. When did you learn anything about Greek dancing?

HARVEY. Maybe not so much the technical aspects of the footwork but more the spirit of the thing, the emotional commitment it demands.

JUNE. God help us.

HARVEY. Theo, I think you should join us. You need a little loosening up.

THEO. I don't really…

HARVEY. I insist, Theo.

ADRIAN. Yes, Daddy!

HARVEY. But put that knife down first, we don't want you dancing with a carving knife in your hand.

HARVEY *moves to the centre of the terrace and stretches out his arms, crossing his legs and clicking his fingers Greek-style.*

JUNE. You look ridiculous.

HARVEY. Come on, kids, get into place, Theo, you too, stand behind me and do what I do.

ADRIAN *and* ROSALIND *run and get into position behind him.* THEO *puts the knife down and joins them too, a little sheepishly.* CHARLOTTE *is annoyed by his participation.*

CHARLOTTE. Theo, what are you doing?

HARVEY. Stretch your arms out like this and click your fingers in tune to the music but do it with some feeling!

*They all do as instructed. The dance begins.*

The main thing is to keep your head up high! You're survivors, you've been through four hundred years of Turkish occupation, and you need the world to know that nothing will ever get you down again!

*As he dances he turns and looks at what the kids are doing.*

Jesus, Adrian, higher, that's four hundred years, not a weekend! Rosalind, bend those knees a little, and get the fire in the eyes, you need the fire, you look like you're from Surrey, England, not this troubled land!

JUNE. I think she's doing well, she looks Greek.

HARVEY. Feel the pain and pride in the music and let it sweep through every part of your body like an electric current!

Adrian, I won't say it again, stick that head up in the air, that's good, Theo, get those hips moving, it's that Middle Eastern influence coming through!

THEO (*gyrating his hips quite suggestively*). Like this?

HARVEY. More, Theo, more, think Egypt, it's not that far away, just across the Med there, think Cleopatra, Theo, think belly dancing, you can do it!

CHARLOTTE *suddenly and quickly moves to the cassette recorder, switches it off. The abrupt action shocks them all into silence for a few seconds.*

ADRIAN/ROSALIND. Mummy! Why did you switch it off!

CHARLOTTE. You're still in your swimsuits, and they're wet, I want you to get dressed for dinner.

ADRIAN. Mummy, please!

ROSALIND. Mummy!

CHARLOTTE. Children, please do as I say.

HARVEY. You don't like our dancing, Charlotte?

ADRIAN. Why can't we dance with Harvey, Mummy?

CHARLOTTE. Children, please.

THEO. It's just fun, Charlotte.

HARVEY. You don't like our dancing? You don't like watching
    your husband shaking his hips like that?

CHARLOTTE. Honestly? No, I don't like it, Harvey, I don't
    like your dancing.

THEO. It's just fun, Charlotte.

    *She ejects the tape out of the cassette recorder, takes it in
    her hand.*

CHARLOTTE. I'm sorry, it's this music, this tape.

HARVEY. What about it?

CHARLOTTE. I'm not going to say it again, children. I
    want you to go and get out of your wet clothes and into
    your dry ones.

    ADRIAN *storms off, into the house.*

ADRIAN. You're horrible!

    ROSALIND *follows him off, both in a tantrum. But* JUNE
    *stops her.*

JUNE. Rosalind, sweetie, can you go get Auntie June's
    cigarettes for her, I've got the shakes all of a sudden. They're
    in a carton, sweetheart, at the bottom of our suitcase under
    all the clothes, just bring me a new pack, sweetie.

ROSALIND. All right.

    *And she goes.*

CHARLOTTE. I'm sorry, I bought this cassette in town, from
    that little shop behind the church.

THEO. So what, Charlotte?

CHARLOTTE. And the young woman in the shop told me
    something about it. I mean, I said I wanted to buy something

Greek and she recommended it to me, and she talked to me about it, I mean about this particular type of music.

HARVEY. Jesus.

THEO. Why does that mean we can't have fun with it?

CHARLOTTE. It's called *rebetiko*, Theo, it's a type of music, and it's called *rebetiko*…

THEO. So what?

HARVEY. I think I know where this is going.

HARVEY *goes and pours himself a glass of the punch.*

CHARLOTTE. It's originally from Asia Minor across the sea there, from the small Greek towns of Asia Minor, and people brought it to Greece when they were forced to migrate here after the war with the Turks and the population exchange that ensued.

JUNE. The cassette, they brought the cassette?

HARVEY. She means the music, June.

CHARLOTTE. Its history is rooted in this part of the world – the Eastern Aegean – and its *soul* – I mean, the place it comes from, Harvey, its *source*, its flame, its ignition, is in people who have little power or money trying to express experiences such as alienation, subjugation, poverty, migration, that sort of thing, you know.

THEO. Like Greek blues?

CHARLOTTE. Yes, Theo, exactly, like Greek blues.

HARVEY. Please tell me you are joking about this.

CHARLOTTE. So I'd rather my children weren't taught to trivialise the experiences of other people, especially those they know nothing about and whose pain they can't begin to fathom.

*Pause.*

That's all.

JUNE. Charlotte, I'm sorry, I think that's overreacting. I mean it was just a joke, and the kids were having fun.

THEO. I do think that's a bit over the top, love.

HARVEY. I wasn't trivialising, or mocking.

*Pause.*

I said to you – well, not to you personally, but to everyone here – that I thought it was fitting to celebrate the fact that Greece is now a democracy and I suggested we do so in a light-hearted and entertaining way. Your response is ridiculous, Charlotte, and melodramatic.

CHARLOTTE. Well, I'm sorry, yes, maybe I am being a little melodramatic but there's something I find innately distasteful about people from one culture appropriating things from another one, and then imposing things onto it which are not even native to its character.

HARVEY. You mean the way Theo was moving his hips?

CHARLOTTE. Anglo-Saxons or whatever we are, sitting here, on this terrace, in this country we don't know all that much about, ridiculing their dancing, and imposing things on them, making them live the way we want them to live, forcing them to be like us.

JUNE. Actually, Charlotte, my ancestors are Swedish.

THEO. Charlotte, I've lost you, what were we forcing them to do, what are you talking about?

CHARLOTTE. And before we start celebrating democracy, Harvey, maybe we should ask if this particular kind of democracy is the one the Greek people had in mind.

HARVEY. Go on.

CHARLOTTE. I'm sure that a handful of Greek families are appreciative of this new democracy, of the way it benefits their Swiss bank accounts, but the real people of Greece – oh, I mean teachers, Harvey, and nurses, and workers, and I don't know, people on the streets, people in the fields –

HARVEY. 'Fields'? Did you actually say '*fields*'?

CHARLOTTE. I wonder if they have as much reason to celebrate as you do, Harvey. Time will tell, I suppose.

*Pause.*

Yes, Harvey, I said fields. It's an agricultural country after all, that much I do know.

HARVEY. You're amazing. She's amazing, Theo.

CHARLOTTE. Thank you, Harvey. But anyway, yes, let's try and imagine what's best for the majority of people, not just a small and favoured elite. Both here, and in Chile.

*Pause. She throws the last word at* HARVEY *with some precision and it lands effectively.*

*Then* ROSALIND *runs on. In one hand she is holding a pack of* JUNE*'s Virginia Slims. In the other she is holding a gun.*

ROSALIND. Mummy! Daddy! Look what I found!

THEO. Jesus, what the fuck...

CHARLOTTE *and* JUNE *scream,* THEO *ducks under a table.*

*In one swift move* HARVEY *moves over to* ROSALIND *and swipes the gun out of her hand. The others are staring in shock.*

HARVEY. It's a work thing.

JUNE. Jesus, honey, I told you not to leave it in the suitcase.

CHARLOTTE *storms over to* ROSALIND *and leads her off the terrace, back into the house.*

CHARLOTTE. Put that thing away, Harvey, I never want to see it again and you should never have brought it into this house in the first place!

JUNE. We're leaving in the morning, Charlotte.

CHARLOTTE *storms off, with* ROSALIND. *An awkward pause.* THEO *is in shock.*

HARVEY. People have been killed, Theo. An attaché at the
Embassy. It's defence, that's all. A precaution.

THEO *just looks at him, uncomprehending, still reeling.*

I'll put it somewhere safe.

*And he leaves with the gun.*

JUNE *stands, starts moves towards the table a little
unsteadily.*

*She grabs the pack of cigarettes that* ROSALIND *has
dropped on the floor, takes one out, lights it.*

JUNE. You guys have been so nice to us, and welcoming, we
really appreciate it. But your wife is quite something, all that
stuff about the dancing, what was that about?

*She then goes to the table, refreshes her glass with punch.*

It's like she doesn't like Harvey, like everything he does and
says annoys her. But then I ask myself, why does she keep
asking us over? Do you know what I mean, Theo?

*Pause.*

Cos on the phone I was like, 'Hi, Charlotte, we're staying at
the Grande Bretagne in Athens for a while,' and she was like,
'Well, you must come over and see us, you must come to the
island,' and she wouldn't take no for an answer.

*Pause.*

So it's not as simple as that, is it, Theo?

*And she looks at him for confirmation.*

THEO. It rarely is, June.

HARVEY *bounds back with a somewhat forced enthusiasm.*

HARVEY. Ammunition safely packed away and the kiddos
are safe!

JUNE. Lucky them. Honey, let me pour you a glass, you need
a drink.

*She picks up the jug of punch and starts pouring. But she accidentally drops it and the punch spills all over the table, and the floor.*

Oh, shit, oh, no! Fuck, shit, fuck!

HARVEY. Jesus, June.

THEO *makes a move.*

THEO. I'll get something to clean that up.

JUNE. No, I'll do it, I'll do it, I made the mess so I'll clean it up, Theo, that beautiful wooden table, and the stone floor. You stay here with Harvey, I'll sort it out, it's all under control.

*And she totters off into the house, almost tripping as she does so.*

HARVEY. She's hammered.

THEO. This place is a mess.

*He starts to tidy up – picking scattered things up from around the terrace and placing them in a corner. HARVEY grabs a lighter from the table and walks around the space, lighting the candles.*

HARVEY. God, Charlotte is angry, Theo.

THEO. Well, she's passionate.

HARVEY. Are you guys okay together? I mean in every way?

THEO. Every way?

HARVEY. Is there anything you feel you want to say to me?

THEO. About what?

HARVEY. You know what.

THEO. Not really.

HARVEY. 'Not really' you don't know what or 'not really' you don't have anything to say to me.

THEO. Both, I think.

HARVEY. Are you sure?

THEO. Yes, I think so.

HARVEY. *Think* so?

THEO. Yes, I do.

HARVEY. Okay.

*Pause.*

It's just I'm trying to figure out why your wife is so angry, you know, wound up all the time.

THEO. Maybe she's just a little confused, Harvey.

HARVEY. Maybe.

THEO. Most of us are, aren't we?

*There's a pause and they stare at each other, holding it for a few seconds.*

Thank you for that eulogy a little earlier, though I didn't recognise the man you were talking about.

HARVEY. Don't say that, Theo.

THEO. You say my work is quietly political but I suspect that's a little like saying something is moderately excellent. A bit of an oxymoron, isn't it?

HARVEY. Is it?

THEO. I'm not quite the same man you met all those years ago. Slowly, imperceptibly, drip, drip, drip, I have made... I make choices which are the easier ones. The ones that demand less of me.

HARVEY. I don't think...

THEO. Oh, I'm successful I suppose, yes, you were accurate in that. And I enjoy that success a little too much. But *important*... I'm not saying I don't have that gift... the one you mentioned... the gift of being able to imagine myself into other people's shoes.

*He thinks about it a little, and it is as if, when he speaks,
he is articulating something for the first time, and for his
own benefit.*

But what is the point of being able to imagine what it is like
being other people, if we never, ever act on it? Oh, you may
be repositioned, Harvey, but the view is always the same,
just from a different angle. Nothing really changes, does it?

*Pause.*

Do you know, I feel as if I don't quite remember who I am.
And that only a strong, sharp shock will be able to remind me.

CHARLOTTE *returns with* JUNE *in tow.* CHARLOTTE *is
carrying a bowl of water and a washrag.*

JUNE. I'm so sorry, Charlotte, I'm a klutz, I just knocked it
over and it went everywhere, I'm such a klutz.

CHARLOTTE. It's fine.

JUNE. Let me do it, give me the washrag, let me do it.

CHARLOTTE *starts trying to clean up the mess, but* JUNE
*gets in* CHARLOTTE'*s way.*

CHARLOTTE. I think I'll just mop it up with water first.

JUNE. It's only fair that I should clean it up, I was the one who
did it.

CHARLOTTE. It's fine, June, it doesn't matter who cleans it up.

JUNE. Oh, and it's on the floor too. Please, I insist, give me
that, let me do it.

CHARLOTTE *snaps.*

CHARLOTTE. It's fine, I'm fine! Just let me do it my way,
June, please!

HARVEY. She doesn't want your help, June, just let her do it,
you've done enough already.

JUNE. It was an accident, Harvey.

HARVEY. Leave it, June. Pour yourself another glass of punch and watch the sun go down.

JUNE. I want to help.

CHARLOTTE. Tell you what, June, why don't you go and get the plates, we can start setting the table for dinner.

HARVEY. Is that a good idea?

JUNE. It's a great idea, I'll do that, thank you, Charlotte.

HARVEY. I know it's a Greek tradition, but try not to break any, sweetheart.

*JUNE goes back into the house. CHARLOTTE is wiping the table. THEO hovers.*

THEO. Do you want… should I?

CHARLOTTE. No, I'm fine, Theo, it's fine.

THEO. Okay.

*There is a slight pause as she keeps cleaning up.*

HARVEY. I feel I need to apologise on behalf of my wife.

CHARLOTTE. You don't need to do that.

HARVEY. She's clumsy after she's had a few.

CHARLOTTE. She's unhappy, that's all.

HARVEY. Wow. You girls have been talking, haven't you?

*CHARLOTTE hands the bowl of water to THEO but holds onto the washrag.*

CHARLOTTE. Theo, can you take this back inside?

*He takes the bowl from her.*

Thank you.

*He takes the bowl inside, leaving CHARLOTTE alone with HARVEY. For a few seconds they don't talk.*

*CHARLOTTE takes a look at the floor, notices the stain that the punch has left. She kneels down, scrubs a little. HARVEY watches her a while before he speaks.*

HARVEY. You don't know anything about Chile, Charlotte.

CHARLOTTE. I know enough.

HARVEY. What you read in your left-wing papers?

CHARLOTTE. Oh, Harvey, come on, you can do better than that.

HARVEY. So what do you know?

*CHARLOTTE stops scrubbing. She stands and looks at him, speaks with precision, and intent, head-on.*

CHARLOTTE. I know that there was a democratically elected government, Harvey. I know that that democratically elected government was aiming to improve the lives and livelihoods of the majority of Chileans and I know that that wish was in direct opposition to the interests of a small number of powerful local families and a clique of American multinational cooperations. I know that all the efforts that the Chilean Government were making to implement real social change – including free health care and education for the very poorest – were thwarted and sabotaged by your own government and by big-business interests, and that that same government was instrumental in bringing about the eventual downfall of the democratically elected Chilean one. I know that many people were tortured and killed in the process. And that many disappeared, Harvey.

*She holds his stare. She holds it for a few seconds, but it's enough.*

I know that your definition of democracy is quite a selective and unique one and that you've been very effective at convincing a large number of people in the world that it's also honourable. I know that it's useful to have an enemy like the Soviet Union – a bogeyman – because you can use that enemy to justify a whole lot of what you do whilst diverting attention from your own crimes and misdeeds and I know that if it wasn't for the Soviet Union, that bogeyman would be someone else.

*She looks him straight in the eye again.*

And I know that at some point soon, you're going to have to stop lying to yourself.

*He moves away from her, goes to the cigarettes, takes one out of the packet, lights it.*

HARVEY. Are you angry with me because I never fucked you, Charlotte?

CHARLOTTE. Don't do this. To yourself, I mean. Hold on to something. If dignity is out of reach, then I'd settle for decorum.

ADRIAN *and* ROSALIND *run on to the terrace, dressed for supper.*

ADRIAN. Mummy, we're ready for supper!

ROSALIND. We're ready, Mummy!

*She kisses them.*

CHARLOTTE. Well done, darlings, we'll be eating in a few minutes.

ADRIAN. Please, Mummy, now that we're in our dry clothes, can we dance with Harvey again?

ROSALIND. Yes, please, Mummy.

CHARLOTTE. No, darling, no more dancing with Harvey.

*JUNE returns from the kitchen, holding a tray with a stack of plates on it, and cutlery. THEO follows her, carrying a plate with some small spinach triangles on it.*

JUNE. Oh my God, look at you two, all dressed for dinner, don't you look adorable, like you're going to church or something.

THEO. That thing's going to take some time to heat up so I brought these spinach thingies to snack on.

*He places them on the table, the kids take one each. JUNE puts the tray down, fills up her glass. CHARLOTTE takes the cutlery off the tray, starts placing it around the table.*

JUNE. I wanna make a little speech now, why should I always be the one left out?

THEO. When do we ever leave you out, June?

JUNE. Adrian, Rosalind, come here.

*The children go up to her. She kneels down to them.*

Auntie June wants to say thank you so much for having us and we love you very much.

*She kisses them, then stands again.*

There, that's my speech.

*She looks across at* HARVEY.

Look at my husband, isn't he a handsome man? A little tired, but still a handsome devil, isn't he, Charlotte?

CHARLOTTE. Very, yes.

JUNE. And I know he's not perfect, but I love him to bits and he's all mine.

*She returns to the plates, starts to place them around the table.*

ADRIAN. Mummy, where are the papers and the crayons?

CHARLOTTE. Wherever you left them, darling.

ROSALIND. In the box!

*She runs over to a box by the edge of the terrace and brings out some paper and crayons.* ADRIAN *follows her, gets some too.*

ADRIAN. We're going to draw the sunset, like we did the other day.

*They run to a spot on the terrace and sit down with their papers and crayons.*

CHARLOTTE. What a good idea.

JUNE (*looking up at the sky*). I hope you've got lots of orange crayons, sweetie, you'll need them. And purple, and lilac, and a pale, pale blue.

*She puts the plates down for a minute, leans over and has a spinach triangle.*

These spinach thingies are so good, they're so yummy.

THEO. They're good, aren't they?

JUNE. They're delicious. Feta cheese, you see, Harvey, say what you like but it works.

*She picks up the plates again, continues to place them around the table.*

These are such beautiful plates, Charlotte.

CHARLOTTE. Yes, you said you liked them the other night, June.

JUNE. They're so special, I just can't get over it. The pattern, and the colours are just so lovely.

THEO. They came with the house.

JUNE. They're beautiful.

THEO. Yes, we were lucky, weren't we. We got all the stuff with the house, the furniture and everything, the plates, and cutlery…

CHARLOTTE. Theo, can you bring the chairs over?

THEO. And those beautiful old iron beds. They all belonged to the grandmother.

JUNE. Well, we were here when it all happened, Harvey, don't forget, we were standing right there.

HARVEY. We were, June, how could I ever forget?

CHARLOTTE. I'll go get the food.

*THEO starts to gather the chairs around the table, CHARLOTTE goes back into the house. HARVEY drifts over to the area where the Polaroid photos are and spots them under the flowerpot. He moves the pot, picks the photos and pages of measurements up, starts looking through them. THEO notices.*

THEO. Oh, that's… em… could you…

JUNE. I'm going to do some Greek cooking back at home, Harvey. I'll try a moussaka, and maybe that macaroni-pie thing we had on the beach. And those little potato cakes you like so much.

THEO. Doubt they'll taste the same in Washington, June.

JUNE. We'll have a Greek night, ouzo on tap.

HARVEY (*holding the photos*). This is a nice one of you, June.

JUNE. Let me see it.

*She walks up, takes it off him.* THEO *comes and looks at it too.*

Oh, it's awful, I look horrible, like a sad, ugly, old woman.

THEO. You don't look sad.

JUNE. Oh, you brute!

*And she playfully pummels him on the arm.*

HARVEY *is looking through the other photos.*

HARVEY. Why have you taken all these photographs of the house, Theo?

THEO *immediately tenses up.*

THEO. Oh, them, they're nothing.

HARVEY. What do you need them for?

THEO. Oh, nothing… they're just, em, they're just for a friend.

HARVEY. A friend?

HARVEY *now looks at the paper with all the measurements of the house on it.*

And the measurements. You've measured everything.

*He reads from the paper.*

'Square footage of front terrace.' 'Wall between door and kitchen window.' 'East-facing side wall.' What's it for?

THEO. Some work that will be done to the house.

HARVEY. You're renovating?

THEO. Well, yes, I mean, not really… but it's more complicated.

HARVEY. What is?

THEO. The thing is…

*He pauses. Throws a quick look towards the house to check that* CHARLOTTE *is out of earshot.*

HARVEY. Go on.

THEO. It's not important.

HARVEY. Tell me, Theo.

*Pause.*

THEO. We have loved it here, Harvey.

HARVEY. That's what your wife said earlier. You *have* loved it.

THEO. But now the time has come to move on.

*Pause as this information sinks in.*

HARVEY. You're selling the house?

THEO. Well, kind of.

HARVEY. Kind of?

THEO. Well, yes. We are. We're selling the house.

*Pause.* JUNE *looks up.*

Not to *anyone*, though, not to strangers. To some people we know. A German couple. They visited last July and fell in love with it. They've made an offer we can't refuse.

HARVEY. I see.

JUNE. You're selling the house, Theo?

HARVEY. That's what he said, June.

JUNE. Oh, that makes me sad.

THEO. Me too, June. But our needs have changed.

HARVEY. Your *needs*.

THEO. It's not easy. With the children, I mean, up and down to Greece. And life is expensive.

JUNE. But you're doing so well, Theo.

THEO. We spent Easter in Cornwall. We happened to find this little cottage at the end of a dirt track, near the cliffs. We rented it but it's up for sale.

HARVEY. How lovely.

THEO. So it's about convenience, really.

HARVEY. Convenience.

THEO. Maintaining this place is difficult. And then, as I say, with the kids. I suppose it's easier to just get in the car...

HARVEY. And zoom it down to Cornwall.

THEO. But it won't be easy. We've spent some of our happiest times here.

JUNE. Of course you have.

THEO. And we can't turn the offer down. It's a lot of money, it will pay for the place in Cornwall and there'll be quite a bit left over.

HARVEY. How much are they offering?

THEO *is taken aback by the abruptness of the question, seems suddenly embarrassed.*

THEO. Best not to talk about it with Charlotte. It's a sore point, she'd rather I hadn't told you.

HARVEY. I'm sure.

JUNE. Of course, we understand, our lips are sealed.

THEO. So maybe let's just change the subject.

HARVEY. Yes, fine.

THEO. Anyway, we were very lucky when we found this place.

HARVEY. Best day of your lives.

CHARLOTTE *returns with a large bowl of salad. She places it in the middle of the table.*

CHARLOTTE. We can start with this and then I'll get the stew after, it still needs a few minutes, that hob is acting up again.

*They all start to sit down.*

JUNE. That salad looks beautiful, Charlotte.

CHARLOTTE. Same as usual. Children, put away the drawing things and come and sit at the table, supper's ready.

ADRIAN. In a minute, Mummy.

JUNE. Our last meal together.

THEO. Indeed.

JUNE. You've been so kind and hospitable. You've made us feel loved. I'd make another speech, but I think I might just start to cry. I don't know why, but I think I might. I feel very sad all of a sudden.

THEO. Let's try not to cry, June.

JUNE. I'm such a softie, especially when I've had a few drinks.

CHARLOTTE. Help yourselves to the salad.

*They all start to help themselves to the food.*

HARVEY. So you're selling the house, Charlotte.

CHARLOTTE *throws* THEO *a look, who in turn stares at* HARVEY.

THEO. Harvey…

HARVEY. I know, I'm sorry, Theo, but no more secrets. No more secrets between friends.

CHARLOTTE. Yes, Harvey, we are. We're buying a house in Cornwall.

We love it down there and it will be good for Theo. It's the perfect spot to write in.

HARVEY. Well, Cornwall's beautiful.

*He moves over to the punch, pours himself a glass. There is a pause as the others continue to serve themselves the food.*

Did you ever enquire about Maria and her father, Theo? I mean about how things turned out for them in Australia?

THEO. Not really, no, I mean the uncle was the only one left on the island but then about three or four years ago he too must have moved away because suddenly he disappeared.

HARVEY. No, he didn't move away, Theo. He died of pancreatic cancer.

THEO *stops what he's doing, as does* JUNE. CHARLOTTE *looks up.*

That's when all those words come in handy – I mean the English words which come from ancient Greek, you realise how many words share that root and it really helps when you're having a conversation with the man on the street. Because, yesterday when we went to the port to get the *Tribune*, I left June in a bar and stopped by the tobacconist's to buy her cigarettes and I asked the guy, I said, 'Where was the man who used to own this shop,' and then he told me what had happened to him but his English was so-so, and every so often he'd say something in Greek and when he said that the guy had died of '*pankreatikos karkinos*', well, I figured, that's pancreatic cancer.

*Pause.*

And then I asked him about Maria and her father too, and if he knew what had happened to them. And as it turned out, he did. His mother knew the family quite well, it's a small community, it's natural. So he told me what happened to them.

THEO. Why didn't you tell us?

HARVEY. Because I didn't want to upset you, Theo. I didn't even tell June, did I, sweetheart?

JUNE. Tell me what?

HARVEY. But now I think that you should know. I think it only right that you should know.

*Pause.*

JUNE. What happened, Harvey?

HARVEY. Well, June, he told me that in the beginning everything had started out okay. Maria and her dad had arrived in Sydney, the father had a job waitering in a Greek restaurant and they were renting a small apartment but that then the father – well, the father had joined up with two other Greek guys and had invested whatever money he had in setting up his own taverna, but they'd got it wrong because the only area they could afford to rent the premises in was – well, it just wasn't the right neighbourhood for that kind of venture, it was full of Oriental people or something, Chinese, I don't know. And then he fell out with one of the guys he'd opened it with, and he was swindled, and from what I understood, he just lost all his savings, and remember he didn't have all that much to begin with, I mean he was quite desperate when he left Greece in the first place, he had to sell the skin off his back for next to nothing.

JUNE. I remember, that poor man.

HARVEY. So then this young tobacconist guy tells me that eventually all this took its toll on his health – well, it does, doesn't it – and that he died – Maria's father died a few years after they arrived in Australia, of some heart thing.

THEO. What happened to Maria?

HARVEY. Well, Maria was alone now, Theo, because by that point her uncle over here had died as well. So she was in Australia, and she was on her own. Apparently, she found a job in a hotel, cleaning rooms or whatever, but she was finding it hard to make ends meet.

THEO. Then what?

HARVEY. Well, then, one day, a couple of years later, the tobacconist's mother got a letter from a cousin of hers in Australia who bumped into Maria one night on a street somewhere in the rougher outskirts of the city. But that was the last time anybody ever saw her so nobody from the island knows what happened to her after that.

*Pause.*

This cousin wrote that on that occasion when she saw Maria for the last time she seemed a little strange, I don't know, lost or something, confused, and that she had said something that the tobacconist's mother had never been able to forget.

THEO. And what was that?

HARVEY. That when her father had died all she had wanted was to return to Greece. It's natural. To come home.

*Pause.*

But that she didn't have a house to return to.

*Pause.*

It's sad. Life doesn't always turn out the way we hope it will.

*There is a pause, and suddenly* JUNE *starts crying.*

JUNE. Oh, God, that girl, that poor baby girl.

CHARLOTTE *turns to the children. She speaks calmly, but resolutely.*

CHARLOTTE. Adrian, take your sister inside, darling. Go into your room, and Daddy or I will bring your supper there.

ROSALIND. We're drawing, Mummy.

CHARLOTTE. Adrian, Rosalind, will you please do as I say.

ADRIAN. But Mummy, we want to eat with –

CHARLOTTE. Don't argue, Adrian. Do it now!

ADRIAN *grabs* ROSALIND *by the hand and angrily leads her into the house, shouting as he goes.*

ADRIAN. What's wrong with you today?

*They go.* CHARLOTTE *turns to* HARVEY *and* JUNE.

CHARLOTTE. I'm sorry, June, but I'd like you and Harvey to leave the house, please. I mean, I'd rather you didn't stay here tonight, I'd rather you left.

THEO. Darling…

JUNE (*through tears*). What did you say?

HARVEY. We're being kicked out, June. I'll go get the cases but you'll need your handbag, where have you put it?

JUNE. Being kicked out?

THEO. Charlotte…

HARVEY. It's August, I imagine most of the hotels are full, but we'll find something and if the worse comes to the worst we'll settle on a bench at the port, it's just the one night.

CHARLOTTE. Get out of this house.

HARVEY. So I'll get those cases now, June, but it would help me a great deal if you could look for your handbag and gather any other things you may have lying around and then we'll call a taxi and get out of your way.

THEO. Harvey, wait, let's just talk…

CHARLOTTE. THEO, NO!

HARVEY. Come on, June, get into gear.

JUNE *stands, but is unsteady on her feet, and emotional.*

JUNE. Why are you kicking us out, Charlotte? What have we done?

CHARLOTTE. I'm sorry, June.

HARVEY. Come on, sweetheart.

HARVEY *makes his way towards the house, then stops, turns to* CHARLOTTE *and* THEO.

It may come as a surprise to you to learn this, but when I heard that news yesterday I had to take a five-minute walk through the backstreets of the port, on my own. You see, I remembered that girl, and all the hope she had, and I…

*But he is suddenly overcome with emotion, his voice breaks
and he stops. He takes a few seconds, then continues.*

I didn't want to tell you, Theo, Charlotte, and that's the
honest truth. But you haven't given me a choice, Charlotte.

*Pause.*

I will carry that boy on my shoulders – the Chilean one, his
music, the way it ended so abruptly. I will carry him – the
full weight of him – and many more like him. But you
should carry Maria.

*Pause.*

You see, Charlotte, if we're going to stop lying, I think it
only fair that we do so together.

*And he walks into the house.*

JUNE *walks unsteadily towards the small bottle of nail
varnish, and picks it up.*

JUNE. I'm sorry, I don't know any more, I just don't understand.

*And she follows* HARVEY *into the house.* CHARLOTTE
*breaks, falling into* THEO's *arms, then pushing him away.
She is hysterical.*

CHARLOTTE. Oh, God, why did we do it, why did we do it?
Why did we do it, Theo?

THEO. We weren't to know.

CHARLOTTE. She said… she had a sense… she tried to stop
us, Theo, she tried to stop us!

THEO. I know, I know she did.

CHARLOTTE. But we didn't listen, we didn't listen, Theo!

THEO. It was my fault, Charlotte, I wanted it so much.

CHARLOTTE. It wasn't ours, it wasn't ours to have!

THEO. We didn't think we were doing anything wrong.

CHARLOTTE. But we were, Theo, we were. We bought the
house for nothing.

THEO. I know, Charlotte, I know we did.

CHARLOTTE. Because they needed it so much, they *needed* it so much!

THEO. We're not bad people, Charlotte.

CHARLOTTE. And I didn't ask, I never asked.

THEO. Asked what?

CHARLOTTE. About them. About what had happened to them. In Australia, or afterwards. I didn't want to know, I didn't want to know, Theo.

THEO. It's all right, Charlotte, it's all right.

CHARLOTTE. I never went near that tobacconist's because I didn't want to know.

THEO. Okay.

CHARLOTTE. She tried to warn us but we didn't listen!

*And she falls into his arms, and weeps.*

*HARVEY returns, carrying two suitcases and a backpack.*

*CHARLOTTE immediately separates from THEO, not wanting to show HARVEY her vulnerability.*

HARVEY. June's make-up is all over the place, she's going to take a few minutes gathering her stuff up.

THEO. That's fine.

HARVEY. But we'll need to order a taxi.

THEO. I'll do it.

*He checks to see if that's all right with CHARLOTTE; she assents.*

*THEO goes into the house. CHARLOTTE walks to the front of the terrace, stares out at the sunset.*

*A few seconds pass before she speaks.*

CHARLOTTE. You know that first evening when you came here, you said that I'd asked you over because I was attracted to you.

HARVEY. I did.

CHARLOTTE. Well, you were right, I was. And I kept asking you back. Even this year, I wanted to see you, I couldn't help myself. I didn't understand it, and I resented it, but I did.

*Pause.*

Now I think it's because I believed what you said that night on this terrace – that you were a good man. And that those things you talked about – those ideals, those values – reason, imagination, questioning, democracy – that all those things you spoke about with such conviction, well, that you were doing what you could to defend them, at great cost to yourself. I believed you, I felt the gratitude you wanted me to feel, and yes, I felt that attraction.

*Pause.*

But not any more. You have forfeited the right to use those words.

*She turns and looks at him.*

And there is nothing else left.

*She walks into the house,* HARVEY *is left alone.*

*For a minute, he does nothing, just stands there, as if allowing the peremptory blows of the words she has just spoken to land on him.*

*Then, slowly, he moves towards the cassette recorder. He looks and finds the Greek tape – picks it up and puts it into the recorder, presses play.*

*The* rebetiko *music comes on and fills the air: mournful, plangent.*

HARVEY *stands straight for a second or two, and listens to the powerful music.*

*Then something happens – his body starts to move a little as if responding to it – his neck, his arm. A tiny movement, but awkward and faltering. It is an instinctive response to the music and the way he moves expresses a profound sense of alienation and despair.*

THEO *comes out.* HARVEY *sees him and immediately switches off the music.*

HARVEY. Still trying to perfect that fucking dance. It isn't easy.

THEO *is terse, unyielding.*

THEO. The taxi will be here in five minutes. And I found you a room in a hotel near the port.

HARVEY. That's kind, Theo.

HARVEY *approaches* THEO *and reaches for him.* THEO *doesn't move. But* HARVEY *perseveres, moving closer to him. He stretches out his arms again, as if inviting* THEO *to embrace him.* THEO *continues to resist. Then, of course, he relents, opens his arms.* HARVEY *falls into them, and sobs.*

*Then, he kisses* THEO *on the mouth. But it is less of a sexual thing, something more ineffable, one person's desperate need for another.*

Don't worry, I'm not a queer. I just love you, is all.

THEO *doesn't know how to reply, so he doesn't.* HARVEY *holds* THEO*'s face in his hands, looks him in the eyes.*

And thank you, Theo.

THEO. What for?

HARVEY. For being loyal.

THEO. Cheese and pickle.

HARVEY *points at the chair, the one he pointed at the end of Act One.*

HARVEY. There she is, in that chair, overlooking her terrain.

THEO. Thalia.

HARVEY. No, not Thalia. Not the Muse of Comedy, Theo. The other one.

THEO. The other one?

HARVEY. Melpomene.

*THEO hovers for a minute, then goes into the house again.*

*HARVEY is left alone. He just stands there, looking at the sunset, his eyes fixed into the distance. He does not move again until the end of the play.*

*A few seconds pass.*

*Then AGAPE walks on. She is an elderly Greek woman and she is wearing simple peasant clothes. She is carrying a bowl of string beans. She is MARIA's grandmother.*

*She comes up to the table and pulls a chair up, sits.*

*She starts stringing the beans, but after she's done a couple she stops, and shouts.*

AGAPE. *Μαρία, Μαρία, που είσαι;* [Maria! Maria, where are you?]

*She carries on stringing the beans.*

*A few seconds later, MARIA comes out of the house. She looks a couple of years younger than when we last saw her, maybe her hair is in a ponytail, maybe she's wearing a school uniform. She is carrying an English textbook, something from school.*

MARIA. *Γεια σου γιαγιά.* [Hello, yia-yia.]

AGAPE. *Που κρύβεσαι;* [Where have you been?]

MARIA. *Τ' Αγγλικά μου κάνω.* [I've been doing my English.]

AGAPE. *Κάτσε να με βοηθήσεις λίγο.* [Sit down and help me for a while.]

*MARIA sits down and starts stringing beans with her grandmother. She speaks to her in English.*

MARIA. I am doing the English homework, Yia-yia.

AGAPE. *Τι λες;* [What are you going on about?]

MARIA. *Τ' Αγγλικά μου.* [My English.]

AGAPE. *Τι τα θέλεις;* [What do you need it for?]

MARIA. My father is saying it is very useful for me to speak the English.

AGAPE. *Τι είναι αυτά που μου λες βρε!* [Listen to you!]

*For a few seconds, they string the beans in silence. Then, AGAPE puts down the beans, and looks out. She is looking in the same direction that HARVEY is, out towards the sunset, and the sea. MARIA keeps stringing the beans, and looking at her English textbook.*

*Maria?*

MARIA *looks up.*

MARIA. *Τι;* [What is it?]

AGAPE. *Τ'αγαπάς αυτό το σπίτι;* [Do you love this house?]

MARIA. *Το ξέρεις ότι το αγαπάω.* [You know I do.]

AGAPE *strokes the side of* MARIA*'s face.*

AGAPE. *Μια μέρα δικό σου θα'ναι. Θα το προσέχεις, μου το υπόσχεσαι;* [One day it will be yours. You'll look after it, you promise?]

MARIA. *Στο υπόσχομαι.* [I promise.]

*And then, in English.*

I promise.

AGAPE. *Το σπίτι.* [The house.]

MARIA. The house.

AGAPE. *Και τα δέντρα.* [And the trees.]

MARIA. And the trees.

AGAPE. *Και την θάλασσα.* [And the sea.]

MARIA. And the sea.

*The End.*

# National Theatre

**The National Theatre** is dedicated to making the very best theatre and sharing it with as many people as possible.

We stage up to thirty productions at our South Bank home each year, ranging from re-imagined classics – such as Greek tragedy and Shakespeare – to modern masterpieces and new work by contemporary writers and theatre-makers. The work we make strives to be as open, as diverse, as collaborative and as national as possible. Much of that new work is researched and developed at the NT Studio: we are committed to nurturing innovative work from new writers, directors, creative artists and performers. Equally, we are committed to education, with a wide-ranging Learning programme for all ages in our new Clore Learning Centre and in schools and communities across the UK.

The National's work is also seen on tour throughout the UK and internationally, and in collaborations and co-productions with regional theatres. Popular shows transfer to the West End and occasionally to Broadway; and through the National Theatre Live programme, we broadcast live performances to 2,000 cinemas in 50 countries around the world. Through *National Theatre: On Demand in Schools*, three acclaimed, curriculum-linked productions are free to stream on demand in every secondary school in the country. Online, the NT offers a rich variety of innovative digital content on every aspect of theatre.

We do all we can to keep ticket prices affordable and to reach a wide audience, and use our public funding to maintain artistic risk-taking, accessibility and diversity.

Chairman of the NT Board **John Makinson**
Deputy Chair **Kate Mosse**
Director of the National Theatre **Rufus Norris**
Executive Director **Lisa Burger**

Box office and information +44(0) 20 7452 3000
National Theatre, South Bank, London SE1 9PX
**nationaltheatre.org.uk**
Registered Charity No: 224223

**www.nickhernbooks.co.uk**

 facebook.com/nickhernbooks

 twitter.com/nickhernbooks